Growing Your Business Online

Growing Your Business Online

Small-Business Strategies for Working the World Wide Web

Phaedra Hise

An Owl Book
Henry Holt and Company
New York

Henry Holt and Company, Inc.
Publishers since 1866
115 West 18th Street
New York, New York 10011

Henry Holt® is a registered
trademark of Henry Holt and Company, Inc.

Library of Congress Cataloging-in-Publication Data
Hise, Phaedra.
    Growing your business online: small-business strategies for
working the World Wide Web / Phaedra Hise.—1st ed.
        p.   cm.
    "An Owl book."
    Includes bibliographical references and index.
    1. Small business—Computer networks.   2. World Wide Web
(Information retrieval system)   I. Title.
    HD62.7.H575   1997   96–22184
    658.02'2'0285467—dc20   CIP

ISBN 0-8050-4738-7

Henry Holt books are available for special promotions and
premiums. For details contact: Director, Special Markets.

First Edition—1996

Designed by Paula R. Szafranski

Printed in the United States of America
All first editions are printed on acid-free paper. ∞
10   9   8   7   6   5   4

To Bill, who always believed I would write a book

Contents

• • • • • • • •

Acknowledgments
● ● ● ● ● ● ● ● ● ● ● ● ● ● ● ● ● ● ●

My biggest thanks go to all of the company owners and managers interviewed for this book, who took time out from running busy, growing companies to share the details of their online experiences so that other businesses can learn.

To my agent, Jane Dystel, thanks for finding the right home for my proposal and attentively following it through the process. At Henry Holt and Company my editor, David Sobel, and his assistant, Jonathan Landreth, deserve my thanks for bringing the book alive and carefully shepherding it through quick publication. Beth Gunn deserves thanks for performing the preliminary interviews for the book, creating a useful database for categorizing them, reporting interesting findings along the way, and sorting through my barrage of E-mail questions and suggestions. Mary Furash worked quickly and thoroughly to gather the appendix information and organize it. It would have been impossible for me to write this book without their help.

To Dave Scobie at Media Bits Web developers in San Francisco (www. mediabits.com/mbits/), many thanks for rounding up the numerous screen shots of Web sites for the book, and creating a convenient Web site for storing them during the process. Thank you to the support staff at my Internet service provider, Software Tool and Die in Brookline, Massachusetts, for cheerfully answering my niggling technical questions at all hours of the day and night, and directing me to other resources when they didn't have answers. A huge thank you to *Inc.* editors David Freedman and Jeffrey Seglin, who were never too busy to answer my questions and dispense advice. Special thanks to my husband, who doesn't know much about the Internet, but certainly knows how to encourage and support me. And finally, thank you very much to Lily Anthea, who was extremely patient and undemanding during the first three months of her life so that her mother could write this book.

Grateful acknowledgement is made to the following: CyberCash used by permission of CyberCash (www.cybercash.com); The List (service providers by zip code) used with permission of Mecklermedia (www.iworld.com); Lycos copyright © Lycos, Inc., all rights reserved; The Lycos™ "Catalog of the Internet" copyright © 1994, 1995, 1996 Carnegie Mellon University, all rights reserved, used by permission; Wordsworth Books used by permission of Wordsworth Books; Avweb used by permission of Avweb Group, Inc.; Aircraft Shopper Online used by permission of Aircraft Shopper Online, Maxfly Aviation, Inc., and Cessna Aviation; Forsyth used by permission of Forsyth Dental Center; IOMA used by permission of the Institute of Management and Administration; White Rabbit © 1996 White Rabbit Toys; Windham Hill: Courtesy of Windham Hill Records® A Division of BMG Entertainment; Yahoo! text and artwork copyright © 1996 by YAHOO!, Inc., all rights reserved: YAHOO! and the YAHOO! logo are trademarks of YAHOO!, Inc.; Dave Scobie's page (Black Planet), all work copyright © 1996 Black Planet; Virtual Vineyards courtesy Net Contents, Inc.; CommerceNet used by permission of CommerceNet; Bibliobytes © 1996 Bibliobytes (http://www.bb.com); Hot Hot Hot used by permission of Hot Hot Hot Online; Eurosport used by permission of Sports Endeavors, Inc.; Virtual Reality Labs used by permission of Virtual Reality Labs, Inc.; Ben & Jerry's Homemade used by permission of Ben & Jerry's Homemade, Inc.; Alberto's Nightclub used by permission of Alberto's Nightclub.

Growing Your Business Online

Introduction

When I first logged on to the Internet as a staff writer for *Inc.* magazine, the Web hadn't been invented yet. Things were pretty ugly. It took me one entire day just to figure out what commands to use for sending email. Despite the difficulty in navigating, I was quickly seduced by the Internet's possibilities for global communication and easy research. During the next year, 1993, I proposed a series of short articles for *Inc.* about online marketing. But while I had no trouble finding companies doing business on the commercial online services—Prodigy, CompuServe, and America Online—it was quite a struggle to find any company doing business on the Internet. I bounced the story from month to month as I searched desperately for any company that was taking advantage of online opportunities. Finally, I settled for a few small companies that were beginning to think about how they might do online sales.

After that series appeared in the magazine, small companies started calling me about their online ventures. Some were doing some creative Internet marketing, a few were setting up online stores on a new section of the Internet called the World Wide Web. I didn't know what the Web was, but it sounded intriguing. Listening to those companies talk about it, I figured the Web must be a colorful, animated shopping mall, sort of like a Saturday morning cartoon that I could walk through with the aid of my computer. But when I finally got there, it was hardly that exciting—it moved a lot slower than a cartoon, and it was certainly more boring. But the surprising thing was that most of the business sites on the Web were from tiny companies—little retail shops, small mail order catalogs, and one-person professional services. It appeared that small business was ahead of big business in testing online commerce. I started paying closer attention. And the Web started looking a lot better and more interesting than Saturday morning cartoons.

When *Inc.* researched the 1995 *Inc. 500* issue, we asked CEOs of America's five hundred fastest growing companies whether or not they had a World Wide Web site, and to our amazement, 20 percent said yes. As I began writing about those companies and others in the monthly Managing Technology column of the magazine, I started hearing from small businesses that knew very little about the Web but were anxious to learn. "What is the Web?" they asked. "How much does it cost to open an online store? How much money can we make? How do we start?" I didn't know the answers, but as *Inc.*'s technology writer, I was determined to find out. Researching the Web and looking for useful resources for busy company owners, I soon realized there was nothing available specifically for small businesses. Although the majority of companies using the Web were small, none of the how-to or online marketing books focused on what small companies were doing on the Web.

This book fills that void—it separates reality from the hype and focuses on how real companies are competing online. I surveyed more than one hundred small businesses ranging in size from under $1 million to $60 million. I talked with manufacturers, retailers, catalogers, and service companies. High-tech companies like software developers still lead the way in creative Web site development, but I also searched for and found low-tech businesses, such as a nightclub, a toy store, and a peanut retailer. Some of these companies were involved in every step of their Web site's development, others outsourced the entire process to industry professionals. I asked them all about the costs, the maintenance requirements, and the payoff of having a Web site. What I learned was that small companies are very excited about the opportunities on the Web. They can set up sites that look as good as or better than their largest competitor. They can make online sales at a fraction of the cost it takes to make retail or catalog sales. They've found creative ways to cut costs while designing creative and entertaining Web sites. And they're investing in future online development, hoping for more explosive growth and exciting business opportunities on the Web.

Who Should Read This Book

Although this book was written for and about small businesses, it will also help managers at large companies that are working with online strategy. The tips in this book can help any company save time and money during the process of developing a Web site. And because the book focuses tightly on *business* Web development, any company can use the information on securing an Internet access account, developing and promoting a Web site, tracking visitors, and performing online transactions. And all businesses that are creating an online presence will be interested to hear what the industry experts predict for the future of the Web and online commerce.

Small businesses in particular will benefit from this book. It is often difficult for small businesses to find information that exists specifically for and about companies their size, because those companies are often reluctant to share hard data about their operations. Subsequently, many small-business owners often feel isolated and left in the wake of large corporations that receive regular media coverage. Those company owners are the audience for this book. Here they will find resources and advice geared for the smaller company on a tight budget. And they'll read profiles of other small businesses that are taking advantage of this new medium in different and creative ways.

Because a large company's marketing budget can be equal to a smaller business's entire yearly revenue, smaller companies are often shut out of glamorous—and expensive—marketing arenas such as television or national publications. Company owners who feel that way about the Web should also read this book. At the moment the Web is open to all budgets, and money isn't the defining factor in creating an exciting and popular Web site. Small companies that follow the guidelines in this book can have sites that are as successful, or more so, than their largest competitors.

How to Use This Book

Because the companies themselves are the primary source for the book's information and recommendations, several short case studies are featured in each chapter. CEOs and managers at small companies that have Web sites talk candidly about their online experiences, focusing on particular points in each chapter.

The book is structured to answer the most common questions I hear from small companies interested in the Web. It follows the natural order of progression: First, learn what the Web actually is, then study how to set up a site and plan how to measure its success, promote it, and decide how it will make money. (A reader who already knows a little about the Web can jump right in at a later chapter.)

Chapter 1 answers "What is the Web?" by looking at it within the context of the rest of the Internet. It dispels some common misconceptions about what the Web is and isn't, and also looks at just how explosively the Web is growing. One company manager profiled talks about his experience setting up electronic storefronts on the commercial online services. Another weighs the costs and benefits of the Web versus a CD-ROM catalog. A third explains why her small business measures up against larger competitors on the Web.

So what's the big deal with the Web? Chapter 2 explains the hype surrounding the Web and why companies should be interested in it. It also describes how consumers use their computers to navigate the Web, and how they find what they're looking for. This chapter shows, rather than tells, what the Web is like by depicting a sample Web site and explaining its different parts. Companies in this chapter have Web sites designed to be viewed by a particular browser software, are set up as online stores in a cybermall, and make smart use of the Web's best feature, hypertext links.

Chapter 3 answers the common question, "How do I get my company online?" by explaining how an Internet access account works and how to get one. It outlines the different types of corporate accounts available and explains how to decide who in a company needs Web access. It also covers the options for limiting access to certain sections of the Web. Case studies illustrate the different kinds of Internet access accounts: One company talks about setting up firewall software, and another discusses limiting employee access to the Web.

Chapter 4 details how to set up a company Web site, beginning with building and storing it in-house on company-owned computers. This chapter explains the advantages and disadvantages to keeping a Web site in-house—and includes a short quiz for deciding if this is the right option for your company. It also covers the equipment required and the steps in designing a site. The companies studied in this chapter illustrate what types of software and hardware to use in building and maintaining a Web site, and one near lawsuit over a site that was copied a little too closely by another company.

An alternate option for building a Web site—outsourcing—is covered in chapter 5. It discusses whether to outsource all or part of the site, and contains checklists to help decide whether or not to outsource at all. As this option is cheaper than building in-house, it's more popular with small companies. Also introduced is the Web's cheapest solution: a combination of outsourcing and building in-house, called a hybrid site. The company profiles in this chapter tell how to find designers, how to create a hybrid site, and how to negotiate contracts with Web site developers.

Chapter 6 is a collection of five small company profiles. Each company's Web site follows a distinct industry model, including an online store/catalog, an intranet site, and an electronic press release. Costs, benefits, profits, and why each company thinks its particular model will pay off are covered here.

Whatever model a company selects, and however the company decides to build and serve its Web site, attracting visitors is the key to success. Chapter 7 discusses setting goals to help measure a Web site's success and smart ways small companies can promote their Web sites. No matter what type of site, there are five essential elements all should have if they're going to attract and entertain Web users. The companies profiled in this chapter follow those guidelines and offer tips on traditional and new promotion methods.

A Web site can offer a lot of statistical data about visitors, and chapter 8 tells how to gather that data with three different Web methods: hit rates, tracking reports, and registration forms. This chapter also includes case studies of companies using all three.

One of the most common questions that company owners ask is, "How do I make money online?" Chapter 9 answers that question by outlining sales and other online transactions available on a Web site. Different transaction options are covered, including encryption software and services. Some types of Web sites make money without making sales, and some save on company expenses. The companies covered here explain how their sites make money.

Everyone has an opinion about the future of the Web, and chapter 10 gathers those opinions together. Industry analysts predict what developments will occur over the next few years in on-line commerce, Web site design, Web structure, legal issues, and more.

Company owners and managers who want to take the next step and start building a Web site can turn to the appendix—a collection of resources, such as Internet service providers that set up corporate Web access, books that explain how to work with specific design software packages, services that offer to handle online transactions, and conferences where Web professionals lecture and demonstrate products and services. Besides a list of books, software, and other traditional resources, the appendix refers to useful Web sites and other Internet resources.

Small businesses are the stars of this new medium, able to move quickly and take risks. I hope that this book encourages your company to explore the World Wide Web and consider the options for your own online site.

1

●●●●●●●●●●●●●●●●●●●●●●●●●●●

What Is the Web?

There's a big difference between the Internet and the World Wide Web. The Web is only a part of the vast Internet, which consists of computers hooked up to other computers via phone/modem lines. In early 1996 there were almost 7 million computers, used by 20 to 40 million people, comprising the Internet. It's tough to get an exact number of users, because some of the computers that make up the Internet are used by more than one person, and some aren't used by anybody. The computers that form the Internet serve different functions. Some of them are just boxes (no monitors or keyboards) dedicated to routing information like email. Some of the computers just store information, such as data files or research studies for people to read or download. Other computers are the personal computers that people use to log on to the Internet.

The advantage to having this tangle of computers hooked up to one another is that no matter where people send email to or from, the message has several different routes it can take. All sent email lists the path it took across the top of the message, along with the sender's email address, the date, and subject. To visualize this routing process, imagine going from one point to another on a spider web. Even taking a pretty direct route, there would be several intersections at which it would be possible to go one of several ways to reach the final destination. On the Internet, each of those intersections is a room where many computers are stored. Those computers are dedicated just to routing email or storing files. These router centers are called Internet "nodes." Every computer that sends or receives email or stores a Web site is connected directly or indirectly to an Internet node.

This seemingly disorganized email routing process is the very reason the Internet was created. In the early 1970s, the U.S. government was experimenting with storing information on computers. Those who were running the experiment realized that storing lots of sensitive data in one physical location posed a huge security risk. So they created four locations, each with a room full of computers, and hooked them together using phone lines that computer modems could use to dial up and connect to the other computers. If one set of computers were destroyed, the other sets could bypass the dead computers and still communicate with one another, sending information along the modem lines via other routes. Someone who wanted to retrieve data could use a computer modem to dial up any of the four computers and copy the files stored there to the connecting computer. This early network was called ARPANET, after its forming agency, the Defense Department's Advanced Research Projects Agency.

Government scientists and researchers working at the different locations began emailing studies to one another from their computers. At the same time, research organizations and companies began connecting their in-house computers via cables to create networks. People began to realize the value of having information stored on one computer accessible from other connected computers. Over ARPANET's large network, huge research files could be stored on one computer, and researchers across the country could instantly access the data without having to store it at their location. Another big advantage of this new government network was that a UNIX computer could communicate with, say, a Macintosh, as long as the networks used the same type of software commands when connecting. The standard for that became Internet protocol, or IP, and people setting up in-house computer networks also used IP. Thus those in-house networks could connect with other in-house networks anywhere in the world that also used IP. This meant that no matter what computers the Department of Energy's network was using, they could still talk with the Federal Aviation Administration's computers as long as they used the Internet to route the email between them.

Universities and colleges soon got involved. In 1986 the National Science Foundation created its own series of fifteen computer centers, or Internet nodes, for routing email and files. This network of nodes, called NSFNET, was connected to ARPANET's computers. The computer centers were basically just rooms that held large computers dedicated to routing email and files. The nodes, located in different cities and linked by modem/phone lines, created a nationwide computer "backbone" for other computers and networks.

Because running the phone lines that connected the nodes was expensive, NSFNET was structured only to create and maintain its own backbone. Local colleges and universities that wanted to connect had to pay to run their own phone lines to the nearest node, which was in turn connected to the other centers. Using this network, any school connected to a node could send information to any other connected school or government organization. This is when the Internet really began to be useful to large groups of computer users.

This arrangement went on for several years, as the Internet developed as a way to send research material around the world. In the late 1970s, large corporations with government-funded research labs, such as Xerox and AT&T, started hooking up their engineering and research departments to the ARPANET backbone. Because ARPANET was still government funded, the professors and researchers using the Internet were dedicated to the free exchange of information; commercialization was frowned upon. Internet etiquette dictated keeping messages short and to the point, since modem lines moved very slowly. This atmosphere remained until the early 1990s.

Meanwhile, out in the real world, students who used the Internet for research projects during school in the 1980s were beginning to graduate. They wanted to continue using the Internet, but the government-funded school accounts were available only to students and teachers. And many of the companies these graduates went to work for didn't have Internet connections either. Until the late 1980s, there really was no way for a consumer to reach the Internet except through a university or organization that maintained or connected to a backbone node.

Then, small Internet service providers (ISPs) started springing up to answer the demand for Internet access. A computer enthusiast, often a recent college graduate who was familiar with the Internet, would buy a computer and modem and would pay to run a dedicated phone line from that computer to one of the Internet's backbone nodes. The ISP started charging consumers who used their modems to call up his computer and hook up to the Internet. When those consumers connected to the online world, there was no pretty point-and-click interface, only a blank screen waiting for commands in the UNIX computer language. Using the Internet was difficult, ugly, and time consuming at slow modem speeds. But people logged on nonetheless.

No central body oversees the Internet, and none ever has. As the Internet was growing, each school or government agency that had some of the Internet's computer routers in their building was responsible for those routers. The phone lines were maintained by the local phone company, which charged the organi-

Browsing through UNIX files before the World Wide Web.

zation that had paid to have them installed. Because access to the Internet was still a government-subsidized free service for the majority of its users, commercial use was restricted. There were no laws regulating it. But the schools and organizations that maintained computer nodes refused to carry any commercial traffic. If, as frequently happens today, someone sent email to Internet users in a cooking discussion group and offered gourmet chocolates for sale on Valentine's Day, that person would have his or her Internet access canceled by whatever ISP maintained it. This kind of thing happened often until the early 1990s. By then, businesses were beginning to see commercial potential in the Internet and wanted to be free to pursue it. Finally, in 1991, an organization formed to help establish commercial traffic on the Internet.

The Birth of Online Commerce

The Commercial Internet Exchange, or CIX, was created in 1991 as a way to guarantee Internet access to commercial traffic. The founding members were heads of large ISPs such as UUNET Technologies and Performance Systems International. A nonprofit organization, CIX opened its own Internet node in Santa Clara, California, and began signing up smaller ISPs all over the country as members. CIX members were guaranteed that their commercial traffic would be accepted and routed over the Internet. The ISP members connected their phone lines to the CIX node and sent all email through that hub.

Pretty soon, CIX was overwhelmed with members, mostly ISPs, interested in selling commercial Internet access. Those members complained that anyone else routing commercial traffic without paying for CIX membership should be shut off from using the node to route commercial traffic. But because no central body oversees the Internet, nobody enforced the noncommercialization rule, and CIX never blocked such traffic. Although NSFNET forbade commercial traffic from traveling along its backbone, the organization didn't have the manpower to look at every message and stop the commercial ones. Many small ISPs with commercial customers just sent their customers' email anyway, and it was automatically routed to its destination without being stopped. CompuServe's online service, which first became available in 1979, had been routing email over Internet phone lines since 1989.

By 1992 there was so much commercial traffic online that the government pulled out of the Internet business. Government funds helped to build the Internet infrastructure, but since commercial use was growing, and ARPANET's charter didn't call for it to develop that aspect of the Internet, development was parceled out to the large, private Internet service providers. Today, the NSFNET still exists, but only to connect schools to the Internet.

The Growth of the World Wide Web

After commerce entered the picture, the Internet started changing quickly, and the next few developments guaranteed that it had a commercial future. The first was the development of the World Wide Web. With all the media hype, it may seem like the Web has been around forever. Actually, it's still an infant, born in 1990 and available to the general public only since 1993. It was first developed by a group of Swiss scientists headed by Tim Berners-Lee at the European Laboratory for Particle Physics (CERN). In late 1990, a prototype of the Web was running at CERN, but it wasn't until 1993 that the software that people use to see the Web became widely available. At that time, only about fifty computers housing Web sites were connected to the Internet. Only two months later, there were two hundred such computers. By early 1996, there were over a million.

As the Web grew, businesses became interested in the new medium, but not many understood how to take advantage of it. In late 1993 a nonprofit organization called CommerceNet was funded to help develop commercial use of the Internet. It was the first group to encourage and help businesses put up Web sites, and developed some of the early Web site development and hosting software. CommerceNet put some of the first business sites on the Web and han-

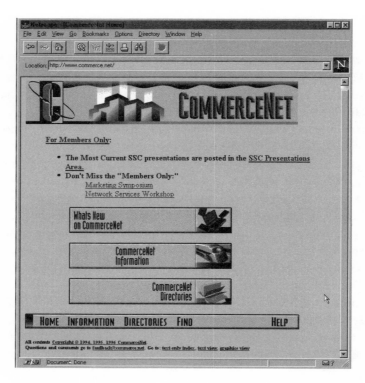

The birth of online commerce. CommerceNet formed in 1993 to pro-
mote online commerce.

dled some of the first online sales. So far, CommerceNet has put hundreds of
companies online and is responsible for businesses and consumers beginning
to see the Web as a new place for commerce.

Today, anywhere from about 20 to 40 million people use the Internet every
day, but that statistic can be misleading. Many of those people are just sending
email along the Internet's phone lines and have never even seen the Web or
other parts of the Internet, such as the online discussion groups known as
newsgroups. As promoters hype the Web as the next big marketing arena, many
studies are using statistics on Internet, Web, and online service users interchangeably. It's easy to get confused, so let's look at some real numbers and see
just what the Web is and what it's not.

The Web Is Not the Internet

If a coworker tells you, "I use Netscape to get on the Internet," she doesn't
really mean the Internet, but rather the World Wide Web. The Web is just a

small *part* of the Internet, with fewer users than the Internet as a whole. While the Internet is made up of almost 7 million computers, routing mail and storing information, the Web is made up of only about 40,000 computers that store Web sites.

Assuming only 20 million people currently use the Internet—the low end of a Nielsen survey's estimated range—that's still slightly more than the 18 million Nielsen says browse the Web. Another study estimates only about 9 million users currently on the Web. Obviously, these studies vary wildly in their estimates and projections of how many people are online and where they go once they get there. No accurate measuring system currently exists. But even though the surveys disagree on the exact number of people hooking up, by 1996 all agreed that the Web still wasn't being used as much as the rest of the Internet.

The Web Is Not an Online Service

However, the Web is being used more than the online services such as America Online, CompuServe, and Prodigy. At the end of 1995, the three big online services combined only had 8 million users—a total less than even a low estimate of 9 million Web users.

Logging on to an online service like CompuServe is not the same as logging on to the Internet. Although all of the online services do connect to the Internet and to the Web, they aren't the same as the Web itself. First of all, each online service has its own collection of activities and information that it offers in addition to Internet access. For example, on America Online, subscribers can type messages to one another live in "chat rooms" that the service maintains. CompuServe has databases of information, such as past issues of many magazines and newspapers, that subscribers can search and reprint. Because there is so much action on the online services, many subscribers don't even bother to venture out into the Internet.

Second, the online services are proprietary networks. This means that every message subscribers send or receive and every site they browse are controlled in some way by administrators. Unlike the Internet, each online service has rules and guidelines about what members can and can't do. (For example, members can't post public messages containing profanity.) Businesses that want to put up sites selling products or services have to negotiate a contract with the online service, often paying exorbitant setup fees and ongoing fees based on a percentage of online sales.

CASE STUDY

Virginia Diner: The Web versus CompuServe

Bill Galloway of Virginia Diner learned the difference between the online services and the Internet in late 1993. The $5 million peanut company based in Wakefield, Virginia, set up its first online catalog with CompuServe in 1992. At that time, CompuServe was recruiting small companies. But Galloway quickly found out that the costs of working with CompuServe weren't worth the benefits.

The company agreed to pay CompuServe a $10,000 sign up fee, and then 2 percent of all online sales. Galloway also paid $5,000 in advance for advertising his company online and in CompuServe's catalog that is mailed to subscribers. Paying the $5,000 up front earned him a total of $10,000 in advertising credits. "We felt really buoyant about it, excited," Galloway remembers. "We started getting a few orders. But we never were privy to the statistics on the number of visitors to the site." CompuServe tracks the number of subscribers who look at the site and what sections they look at but doesn't report those useful numbers to the retailers.

Galloway says he would have liked a larger display space on CompuServe. "We never had our full product catalog displayed, and we only had one item a month featured in color." Galloway was also disappointed with the lack of advertising support. Virginia Diner ads were frequently bumped to later months in the magazine. For example, when the peanut company wanted to feature special Christmas prices, the ad didn't run until January. Basically, Galloway felt that as a smaller company, his company couldn't compete with CompuServe's larger customers. "When CompuServe signed on the bigs of the retail industry, like L.L. Bean, those companies could demand certain things because they have the money to," Galloway says. "It bucked us out of position."

After a year, Galloway began to reconsider his online catalog. "We just couldn't afford it anymore." Then he discovered the Internet, when a local service provider offered to develop a

Web site for the peanut company. In 1993, Galloway finally left CompuServe for the Web. During the next two and a half years, Galloway spent about $40,000 on Internet expenses, including fees paid to the service provider for companywide Internet access, Web site development and storage fees, and long-distance phone charges to connect to his service provider. He's happy with the return that investment has earned. Repeat business online outshines the return on his paper catalog, Galloway says. Online repeat business is at 12 percent versus 10 percent from the paper catalog, and Galloway doesn't have to pay anyone a percentage of his sales. Unlike on CompuServe, he has software that tracks and tells him how many people visit the site daily and what they're looking at before buying. Instead of being limited to displaying a few products, he can put his entire catalog online, with as many color photographs as he likes.

When Virginia Diner opened their CompuServe site, the online service was still recruiting small businesses to open online shops. Now, however, CompuServe and the other online services prefer to strike deals with larger, more established retailers. That's fine with Galloway, who now has more control over his online catalog and more potential customers who see it. "CompuServe has three million subscribers," he says. "The Web has twenty-five million."

The Web Is Not Multimedia

Although Web sites are full of sound and vision, they're not the same thing as multimedia CD-ROMs. There's a distinct difference between debuting a catalog on a Web site and stamping out a few hundred compact discs to mail to customers. Unlike a disc, a Web site can be updated at a moment's notice to list new products or to feature special prices. And unlike a disc, a Web site doesn't have to be shipped to customers—instead, customers go to it. And unlike a disc, which can cost one hundred dollars for every thousand printed, a Web site only costs thirty dollars a month to maintain and can be viewed by thousands of people per day.

Consumers are more interested in the Web than in multimedia CD-ROM, according to an industry survey. Multimedia growth has slowed considerably during recent years. After two years of over 300 percent growth, the multimedia industry expanded at only about 20 percent in 1995. Early that same year, consumer purchases of multimedia computers actually declined.

CASE STUDY

TSI Soccer: The Web versus CD-ROM

TSI Soccer, a $12 million soccer product cataloger, had already started designing a CD-ROM catalog of their products in the spring of 1994. But after comparing that investment to the costs and benefits of a Web site, CEO Evan Jones chose the Web instead.

"The way we saw it, we felt like any customer who'd use a CD could also use the Web," Jones says. "We figure the Web will develop so that eventually CDs won't be that important to people."

With a CD, Jones would have had to update it and mail it to his 50,000-name list every three months. For each update, he'd have to create a new master disc at a cost of $1,000. That included about five hundred photographs, text, and some audio. Add ten cents per disc to produce them, and fifty cents per disc for mailing, and the total cost shoots up to $31,000, not including production labor. The cost of mailing those four times a year averages about $2,600 per month.

By the fall of 1995, the Durham, North Carolina–based company had a Web site up and running at a cost of about one-fifth of a CD. Jones pays his Internet service provider $500 per month to store the Web site on their computers and make sure that it's always accessible to customers. Even including production labor costs, the per-month costs are still lower than those of a CD. A TSI staffer works part-time updating the site and adding new products and prices, at about $1,500 per month, for a total of $2,000. "We can't do all the audio things you can do on a CD," says Jones. "But we can change our catalog instantly without all the mailing costs."

What about the payoff of a Web site versus CD? "We get a lot of visitors to the site, but they don't all turn into sales." Currently, about 15,000 people visit TSI's site each month, and 1,000 request printed catalogs. "We'll keep the site a few more years and see how it develops," says Jones. "The expense isn't that high, and you hate to have a whole new medium out there that starts to take off and you're not involved."

The Web Is Growing Astronomically

The number of Web sites doubles every three to five months. Obviously it won't be much longer before these graphics-rich and easy-to-use Web sites attract even more people. Studies predict that by the year 2000, the Web will have anywhere from 22 to 52 million users accessing it either through standard Internet access accounts or through online services like CompuServe and America Online. Compare that to projections for users of online services alone—only about 9 million by 1999.

Web users appear to come from an attractive demographic profile for advertisers. Commercial users (as opposed to college students or government employees) are logging in at record rates. InterNIC, an organization that registers new Internet users and their email addresses, says that by July 1995 they reported more than 76,000 commercial Internet addresses—compared to only 17,000 a year earlier. Ten thousand new consumer and business users signed on in May 1995 alone. In 1995 for the first time ever, commercial users outnumbered government, educational, military, and other noncommercial users combined. Commercial Web sites—those where companies sell products or services—are also growing astronomically. In less than a year, from September 1994 to May 1995, the number of commercial sites increased tenfold, from about 600 to 6,000.

With commercial Web sites and commercial users logging on at such impressive rates, the Web has quickly become the place to be for business. The rest of the Internet still frowns on commercial activity. Unwary advertisers are rebuffed with harsh "flames," or attacks via email. Most of the users of the rest of the Internet are just hanging out, chatting with friends, or gathering research material. We'll discuss later how to carefully market in some of these areas, but for most businesses, the Web is the only place to be. Consumers visit the Web to be entertained and to buy. Small businesses, able to move and react faster than large corporations, are learning how to do both very well.

The Web Is a Great Opportunity for Small Business

A few years ago, *The New Yorker* ran a cartoon of two dogs sitting in front of a computer. One is typing while he tells the other, "On the Internet, nobody knows you're a dog." Similarly, on the Web, nobody knows you're a small business. The difference between a bad Web site and a good Web site isn't money, it's creativity. Setting up a good Web site isn't prohibitively expensive, so small company sites can look just as good, or better, than large company sites. Because small businesses are frequently leaner and hungrier than their larger competitors, they're more likely to take a chance on a new Web site design or feature. And smaller companies can move quickly, able to make changes without calling endless meetings or securing departmental approval. On the Web, taking chances and moving quickly pays off. Creative, flexible sites attract the most visitors, who then tell their friends to have a look. The Web is one of the few marketplaces where being small isn't a liability, it's an asset.

CASE STUDY

Clam Associates: Competing with Larger Companies

"To me the big thing is the fact that you can get your name known," says Kathy Santos of Clam Associates in Cambridge, Massachusetts. The Web is a perfect marketing medium for this $10 million company that sells software to help recover computer-crashed data. "We compete with large companies like IBM, and the Web doesn't cost that much, so our site can look as good as IBM's. It's not like an ad in *Time* magazine, which IBM can afford and we can't.

"On the Web, when someone searches for disaster recovery software, they find us and also IBM. Our products don't look like products from a small company. They look like products that will solve the problem. By the time the customer finds out we're a one-hundred-person business, they're already familiar with the product. You don't have to work to get your foot in the door with someone who's never heard of Clam."

■　　■　　■

So the Web is only a part of the vast Internet, but it's the part of the Internet that's the most interesting to business. That's because it's the only part of the Internet where commercial activity is welcomed and encouraged, and the only part where consumers go to make online purchases. For that reason, the Web is growing at an astronomical rate, much faster than the rest of the Internet or the commercial online services. Now that this chapter has explained what the Web is, chapter 2 will detail how the Web works by showing how to get there using a computer, what to do once you're there, and what a Web site looks like.

2

• •

How It All Works

It's difficult to describe the Web to someone who hasn't seen it. Using jargon only confuses things further, as in "I got a pointer from Yahoo!, then I jumped to the site and linked over to a mall, where I browsed the listings and loaded a bunch of URLs onto my hotlist." Makes perfect sense to someone who's been using the Web. Makes no sense at all to someone who hasn't. So instead of tossing terms around, we'll explain exactly what it all means.

Just Browsing

It all starts with software—called "browser" software—used to "see" the Web. Netscape, Mosaic, and Chameleon are a few sample software packages. Some work on computer networks, some work only on individual personal computers. The online services like Prodigy and CompuServe offer several different types of Web software.

Browser software is widely available for free. Many software companies and online services send out disks of browser software in promotional mailings. Mosaic and Netscape can be downloaded for free from the Web itself. Free trial disks are available by calling an online service, or one of the larger Internet service providers such as Sprynet or PSInet (see the appendix for a list of service providers). Using any browser software to log on to the Web, users can then download whichever browser they'd like to try just by visiting the Web sites.

A Web user loads the browser software onto his or her computer, programs the modem to call an ISP, and then opens the browser software by clicking on it. The software immediately connects to a pre-programmed Web site. Usually, this default site is programmed into the software by the developers. (For example, Netscape automatically connects to, or "loads," Netscape's own Web site every time a user opens that browser.) Users can change that default setting easily and program the software to automatically load whichever Web site they like when they open, or "launch," the software.

Before there were graphics on the Web, people used text-based "shareware," or free browser software like Lynx and Cello, to view the Web. It looked pretty bad—just black-and-white text—and few companies were impressed enough to put sites online. Then the Mosaic explosion hit. In August 1992, graduate students at the University of Illinois in Champaign-Urbana developed the first browser software, which they called Mosaic, that let users see color graphics on the Web. In the spring of 1994, the university began licensing the software to companies like Spry and Quarterdeck to sell to consumers. Quickly, Web designers started putting graphics on the Web sites they built, since users could see them. Suddenly, it seemed, everyone was talking about how exciting and colorful the Web was.

More history was made when one of the developers, Marc Andreessen, left the university in 1994 to cofound Netscape Communications Corporation. The company established market share by handing out their Navigator software for free, in the hopes that if the majority of consumers were using the browser, then

What a Web site looks like without graphical browser software like Mosaic or Netscape.

more businesses and Web designers would want to buy a product that Netscape charges for—Web site server software, used to create and maintain Web sites. So far, the strategy has worked, and by 1996 Netscape owned more than 75 percent of the browser market. Most Web sites are able to track which browsers are being used when visitors log on, and most of those browsers are Netscape's.

Netscape's market leadership has been a heavy influence on the Web as browser software has evolved because different browsers "see" the Web in different ways. If a site was designed for Netscape, anyone with a Netscape browser will see it exactly the way it was designed: with the correct background color, copy in the correct columns, and graphics in the right position. But the same site will look slightly—sometimes radically—different when viewed with the various browser software packages. Someone logging on with another browser like Mosaic or Chameleon might see, for example, just a plain gray background instead of a yellow one, or text all in one block instead of in columns. Because of this difference, Web site developers must decide which browser software they're going to design for. Although most developers still try to create sites that can be viewed with any browser (testing the site with several browsers before debuting it on the Web), software is getting increasingly specific. It's becoming harder and harder to design a site that works for all browsers, and eventually, one browser is likely to emerge as the industry standard. By grabbing the majority of the market, Netscape has ensured that most of today's Web sites are designed just for it.

The special three-dimensional effects of the programming languages Java and VRML (virtual reality modeling language) are becoming more popular on the Web. With browsers like HotJava and Netscape Navigator that can see the special effects, Web users can see sites that are three-dimensional. A site might look like a small room with doors to walk through, into other rooms. Instead of clicking on buttons or text to experience special effects or move around, Web users are able to click on parts of the room, like file cabinets, windows, lighting fixtures, and stereo systems. Graphics can be programmed to move or change color. Before these special effects become universal, technical problems must be overcome. The biggest is making higher-speed modem connections available so that the effects don't take so long to appear.

CASE STUDY

October Films: Designing for Netscape

"It all came down to graphics," Webmaster Jason Cassidy says. He chose to design his company's Web site specifically to

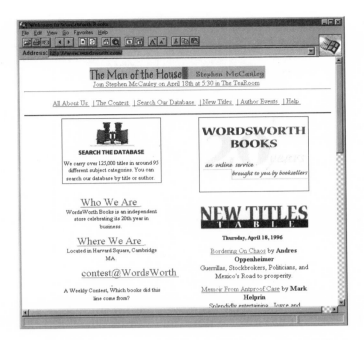

Wordsworth Books' Web site, like most other Web sites, looks very different depending on which browser software is used to "see" it.

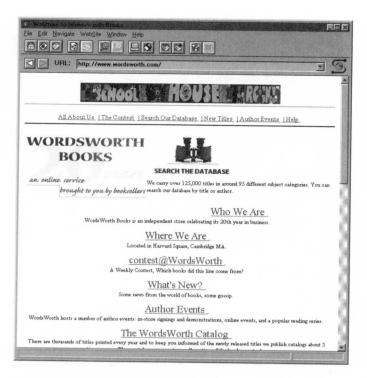

Wordsworth Books' Web site (continued).

be viewed by Netscape Navigator. October Films is a small art-house film distributor, and quality reproductions of the film posters is key to promoting them. Creating a Web site is often a struggle between the desire to use the latest design technology and the reality that not all Web browsers will be able to view it. Rather than compromise his site's artwork, Cassidy chose Netscape, the industry leader, and designed just for it.

"We wanted to enable the most people to use the site effectively." By choosing one browser software to design for, Cassidy was able to keep the film images as true to the original art as possible. If he had designed a site to look the same to all browser software, Cassidy says, "We would have had to do more of a text-intensive site, and that's hard to do for our purposes. We're very image oriented."

Visitors using other browsers can see the site, but just not as well, Cassidy says. "I've been disappointed looking at the site with other browsers." Text doesn't flow around graphic images cleanly, and text stays in one huge block instead of falling into columns. After Cassidy saw that, he did what most companies that design for a particular browser do—put a disclaimer on the site. October Films's disclaimer says that it looks best when viewed with Netscape.

"We've talked about Java's possibilities," Cassidy says. But he won't be working with it, or any other special design features, until the majority of his site's visitors have more sophisticated browsers and are interested in seeing something new. Customers, and not new software capability, will drive the site's design elements. "We'll only act as a reaction to consumers' use of the product. If not a lot of people are using browsers with Java technology in them, we won't be putting those in there."

A Typical Site

Now let's look at a sample Web site as it appears when loaded with a Web browser and explain what's what. This is the first page of IOMA's (the Institute of Management and Administration) Web site, where there is a large collection of business resources and links to other helpful business sites on the Web. The address that users type into the browser software to jump to different Web sites is called the Uniform Resource Locator, or URL. Each Web site has a different URL. In fact, each *page* of each Web site has a different URL. For example, you can type in the URL for the main page of the IOMA site. Or, if you've visited the site several times and prefer to jump immediately to the page that lists resources targeted to small business, you can type in that page's URL the moment you log on to the Web to go directly to that page.

The URL is often a confusing string of nonsense characters, some of which might be part of the name of the site, the name of the computer where the site is stored, and the name of the developer or service provider who created and maintains the site. In this case, IOMA's URL is http://www.ingress.com/ioma/. Let's break that down and see what it means: The first element—http://—stands for "hypertext transport protocol," which is how HTML (hypertext markup language, the programming language used to design Web pages) is sent over the Internet phone lines. Basically, this tells your computer to get into HTML mode and look for HTML information instead of looking

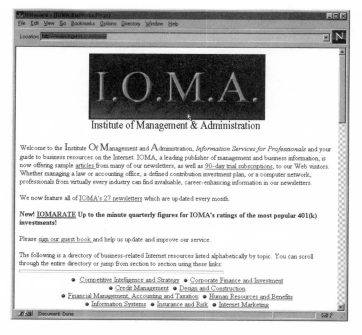

The Institute of Management and Administration has one of the best collections of links to other business sites on the Web.

for something like email or data files. The colon is just a visual separator to make the address easier for us to read and type. The slashes tell the computer that a computer name and address are to follow. Since this part of the URL appears every time, some new browsers automatically insert it so users don't have to.

The next section—www.ingress.com—tells the Web browser's computer what computer name to look for. The field is narrowed from the end to the beginning—"com" tells the computer to search among all the commercial sites stored on the Internet's computers. "Ingress" tells it to look among those commercial sites for only the ones on Ingress's computers, the company that designed and maintains this particular Web site. Most Web sites also have "www" at the beginning, which further narrows down the search to the Web site files on that computer, as opposed to the company's email or other files.

The final narrowing of the field—/ioma/—tells the computer to locate the IOMA Web site, instead of another company's Web site on those Ingress computers. Sometimes there will also be a string of additional letters or numbers, separated by slashes, after this part of the URL. Those are small computer programs that run when a visitor goes to the site. For example, if the site sells products there might be a computer program that tracks which products a customer selects to buy. When that customer goes to the "order" page, the software program automatically fills in the products the customer has selected.

Some URLs are easier to remember than others, and companies are eager to secure a simple URL so that customers are likely to remember it and revisit often. A URL like IOMA's is a little awkward and difficult to remember. It's not always possible to get a simple URL like "www.mycompany.com" or "www. myproduct.com" because another company may have already registered it. Once someone registers a name, no other company or consumer can use it. The service provider usually decides what this name will be. (More on securing a good URL in chapter 4.)

Hitting the Links

Web sites are also sometimes called Web pages, with the two terms used interchangeably. But each site is actually made up of several pages, all layered behind the first one. When visitors click on different graphics or highlighted text on the first page, they jump to the subsequent pages or to other Web sites altogether. The effect is like walking through a series of doors—people can go forward or backward, but they can only be in one room at a time. An example of a connection to other pages at IOMA's site is the underlined blue text that reads "90-day trial subscriptions." Clicking on this with a mouse sends visitors to the page that outlines subscription rates for IOMA publications. On the Web, any blue underlined text is a connection, or link, to somewhere else.

The Web is bursting with colorful illustrations, designs, and sounds. Often, these graphic images are also links to other places within the site or to other sites. Those links are the thing that makes it all work, and what experienced Internet users got excited about when the Web was first created. Links are a useful way to organize information, accessible just by clicking on a word or an illustration that relates to it. This is what the Web hype is all about. With links, visiting a Web site is completely different from other ways people have traditionally gotten information.

Most sources of entertainment and ways of tracking information are linear—that is, you begin at one point and progress through a set pathway until you reach the end. In searching for a newspaper article on microfilm, for example, it's impossible to jump directly to it. Instead, you must begin at the start of the microfilm roll and progress through until you find the article. Television programs, films, and amusement park rides are structured the same way—

everyone begins at the same point, usually at the same time, and ends at the same point after a fixed amount of time.

But the Web isn't linear. It's multidimensional, which means that users begin and end wherever and whenever they like. One user will read through a page of text about scuba diving and click on a link that connects to a site about vacation spots. Another will read through that same page of text, or perhaps only part of it, and jump immediately to a link that connects to a page about training for certification. Sites can be configured so that when a user clicks on a link that connects to a page listing computer printers for sale, an ad appears for that week's specially priced printer. Browsing the Web is a nonlinear experience, customized for each particular user. The Web is unlike any other form of media available before: It ennables advertisers to use a new kind of one-to-one marketing tactic to focus each user's experience.

But because this media is so new, and its nonlinear way of getting information is still somewhat alien to most, many companies with Web sites haven't quite caught on how to use it well. Many are still using traditional forms of marketing and simply presenting information on the Web, like putting up lists of products. Smaller companies seem to have the edge in creative uses. For example, instead of just putting up a price list, many small companies also provide a software program that lets visitors type in the name of the product they're looking for, instead of having to browse through an entire product category.

The Two Types of Links

There are two different kinds of links—internal and external. An internal link leads browsers further into your company's Web site by connecting them to its other pages. So, although users are jumping around and being interactive, they're staying in your company's site instead of leaving. A link that leads users from a product listing to an order page is an example of an internal link.

External links lead browsers away from your site to another site altogether. An example of an external link is one that points from a product list to a product manufacturer's Web site. Users can easily return to the first site by clicking on the "back" key that's part of their browser software (which returns them to the most recent page viewed). But as with any type of advertising, once a person wanders away, there's little chance they'll come back. This is especially true of the Web, with its endless array of tempting links: Users tend to press on and on instead of swinging back. More on external versus internal links, and the correct balance to strike, in chapter 7.

Linking to other sites on the Web is a free-for-all. With a link, Larry's Golf Supplies can point from his site to America Vacation Travel's site without even contacting them and asking permission. Usually, the travel agency would be happy to have that kind of link, because it might bring a few more visitors to their site. Where things get tricky, however, is when Larry wants the travel agency to point from their site to his with a link, sending people away from the travel agency at the click of a button. Larry wants that kind of link because it brings him more visitors. If the travel agency site is really popular, Larry wants that link even more—out of the thousands of people who visit the travel agency site, a few hundred might click on the link that connects them to Larry's Golf Supplies. The agency, however, might not want to give Larry that link—maybe they don't think his site is good enough to recommend to their visitors. Or maybe they don't mind, but they want something in return from Larry for sending their visitors from their site to his. That kind of pointer or link, from a very popular site to a less popular one, usually involves money. (For more details on paying for links and other types of online promotion, see chapter 7. For information on selling links, and other ways of making money online, see chapter 9.)

Searching the Web

The way that Web users find sites like IOMA's or TSI Soccer's amid the myriad other sites is to use one of several indexing software programs, available at certain Web sites. The indexers, also called search engines, regularly canvass the Web and gather the names, addresses, and descriptions of any new sites. Web developers also register new sites with the search engines. Then they index those by name and several keywords, and find them again by matching the keywords that users input. Someone looking for information about airplanes would type *aviation* or *airplanes* into the keyword window of an index program. Then they'd click on the Search button, and the software takes a few seconds to whip through its list, looking for sites that match those terms. Then the search engine jumps to a screen that lists the names of the sites it found, a brief description of each site, and a total of how many there are. The Web user can then browse that list, scrolling down the screen. Just clicking on one of the names on the list immediately connects the user to that site.

Some popular search engines are Yahoo!, Webcrawler, InfoSeek, and Lycos. Some search engines comb only the Web for matches. But InfoSeek and Yahoo!, for example, look through the rest of the Internet as well, locating

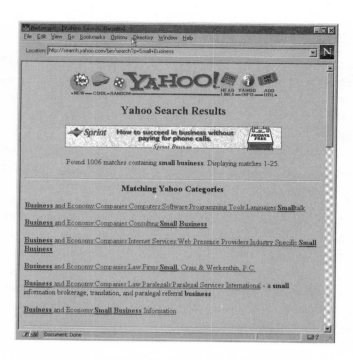

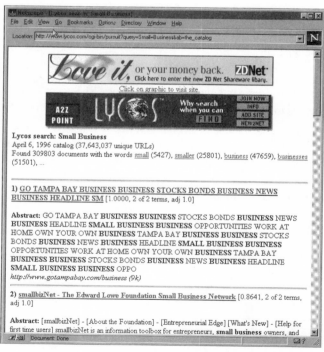

Popular search engines Lycos and Yahoo! enable Web users to find the sites they want.

Internet discussion groups that match. What the search engines look for is keyword matches: Each Web site has a secret section—not visible on the screen—for a listing of keywords that describe the site's content. This section is programmed when the site is first listed with the search engine. For example, a site that sells corporate airplanes might list *aircraft, sales, flying, corporate,* and *pilots* among its keywords. Each time someone uses a search engine and types in one of those words, this site will pop up on the listings shown after the search. Because so many users rely on search engines to find Web sites, using good keywords to describe the site becomes essential in attracting visitors. (More on this and other forms of inexpensive promotion in chapter 7.)

CASE STUDY

Hogs Head Beer Cellars: Browsing the Web's Search Engines

"I didn't really look at the Web because I was just too busy, and I don't gravitate naturally toward playing with a computer," says Polly Nelson, cofounder of Hogs Head Beer Cellars. Despite her low-tech tendencies, Nelson agreed that her company should have a Web site. "Everybody was talking about it, and the Web developer's proposal was reasonable." After the site went up, she discovered the search engines.

"I felt pretty lost, actually," she says about her first time logging on to the Web. After her beer-of-the-month-club site debuted, the Greensboro, North Carolina–based company's Web developer showed her how to use browser software and log on. Although Nelson wasn't immediately comfortable with the new medium, she quickly learned how to navigate.

"What I first started doing was playing with different search engines," she says. She found her own site and competitors' sites easily enough, but "the little descriptions of the different pages where I could go seemed too short—it was frustrating." Nelson fared better navigating from site to site, she says. "Everybody has links, and their links have links." Having a company Web site was what pulled her online. Now Nelson logs on every day for email orders and to look at other beer sites. "It's pretty neat to be able to just pull up what a competitor is doing instead of trying to find out where they're advertising," she says. And she felt comfortable enough to take on a job that her Web developer was doing—listing the company's site with the search engines. "Why pay him when I can do it?" she asks.

Cybermalls

Another way that users find sites they like is by browsing cybermalls. Like regular malls, these cybermalls are large Web sites where several shops are gathered together. Usually the sites have something in common—the same type of product or service or the same geographic location. Visitors to the online version of a mall will find either lists of the shops or icons representing each shop. Clicking on the name of the store or its icon links immediately to the shop.

There are advantages to locating a Web site within a cybermall. Most malls have an "anchor site," just as a real mall has an anchor store. Other shops benefit from the traffic the anchor site attracts. The online malls advertise to draw visitors, which boosts traffic for small shops with limited advertising budgets. Because many malls are run by Web developers and server companies, they may offer bundled site development and maintenance services. For a monthly fee, most malls offer to process online sales, which can be too expensive for a smaller company to offer on its own. If the mall specializes in a particular industry, the developers are already a step ahead of other Web site creators in understanding how the companies in that industry work; it should take them less time to create quality sites for those companies.

Although industry analysts at first expected malls to dominate the Web as it became more crowded with sites, this hasn't happened—mostly because of search engines, which enable users to find whatever they're looking for by keyword. There's really no need for visitors to rely on their favorite mall to find worthwhile sites, so many companies don't bother paying an extra monthly fee to be part of a mall. Another disadvantage of listing with a mall is that companies have no control over what other companies are next door. Perhaps the other sites in the mall are a good fit and attract a good demographic. Perhaps not.

C A S E   S T U D Y

Personal Creations: Setting Up Shop in a Cybermall

When Julie Bridge set up a Web site for her Willowbrook, Illinois–based company, Personal Creations, she chose Evergreen Internet Cybermart mall to create and maintain it. What impressed the $5 million gift item catalog company most was that Evergreen had already landed the catalog giant, Spiegel. "We were really looking for someone who had experience with a catalog company," Bridge says. "Some developers we spoke to hadn't even done online sales." Bridge found Evergreen by cruising the Web and noting what companies had developed sites for the major catalogers.

Bridge signed a six-month nonexclusive contract with Evergreen, specifying that if she eventually leaves the mall, she can take all elements of the site with her to a new mall or server company, except for the online sales capability. She paid $4,700 in October 1995 for a thirty-one-page site, including $900 for use of the transaction software. Evergreen will add pages at a cost of usually about $100 per page, which includes scanning in some graphics and a company logo. Bridge pays $12.50 per page per month to be in the mall. In return for that fee, Evergreen forwards customer email from the site and makes text changes to the site.

The anchor store concept pays off for Bridge. "Somebody comes in to see Speigel and decides they want to see what our site is about," she says. Of the total visitors that stop by Personal Creation's site, 70 percent come from outside the mall, 30 percent come from within. That 30 percent is more visitors than the company would receive if they opened up shop outside the mall.

The One-Hour Browse Rule

Browsing is the key to learning the Web. Because the Web is a new medium, it is impossible to grasp how other companies are using it without going online and checking it out. Before putting together an online strategy, before making changes in that strategy, before putting a site online, before making any decision concerning your Web site, you should spend *at least* one hour browsing the Web. Once you put a site online, you should spend at least an hour a week on the Web. This is essential to creating and maintaining any Web site because the online world changes with lightening speed. What is cutting-edge one week is old hat the next. This is the One-Hour Browse Rule to photocopy and tape across the top of your computer monitor:

> I will spend at least ONE HOUR a week browsing, with an additional hour for every change I plan to make to my Web site.

It may sound time-consuming, but the Web is moving and changing quickly, and visiting it regularly is the only way to keep up. Here's what to look for when you're surfing:

- What links are companies using? Where do they go (internal or external)? How many are there per page?

- What do my competitors' sites look like? How often are they updated? What does the customer feedback page look like? How easy is it to order goods or services? What graphic tricks are they using? Are the sites easy to move around in?

- What do sites look like when viewed with different browsers? How bad do some of the special effects look with the "wrong" browser? How long do sites take to download, and how long am I willing to wait for them?

- How do the different search engines work? What kind of sites do I turn up using different keywords? What keywords should I use to describe my site, and what sites do I turn up if I search on those keywords?

With the One-Hour Browse Rule, you'll learn how your customers will find, see, and use your site. You'll see the latest design developments as they are implemented, instead of just reading about them in a trade publication. You'll learn tricks and shortcuts. If you don't have the time to spend browsing, designate someone in your company to do it for you. Otherwise, you'll end up with a stale, static site that bores visitors. And a lonely site quickly becomes a dead site, with no payoff for the company.

■   ■   ■

To summarize, here's what we have on the Web so far. Growing numbers of consumers and companies are browsing and setting up sites on the Web. Consumers are using search engines to find the sites they want. They're impressed by colorful graphics and jump from site to site using hypertext links. They're visiting cybermalls and shopping online. Companies creating sites are swapping links with other sites and are deciding what links are worth paying monthly fees for. They're making sure their sites are listed with the Web's big search engines so consumers can find them, and they're deciding whether to locate their stores within a cybermall or to let them stand alone.

Now let's look more closely at those companies and how they're getting on the Web in the first place. Chapter 3 will explain who in the company needs an Internet account to help plan and implement the Web site, what kind of Internet access those employees should have, how much it costs, and who provides it.

3

● ●

Getting Around

To follow the One-Hour Browse Rule outlined in the last chapter, at least one person in the company has to have Internet access. Small companies with few employees may want everyone to have access. Mid-size companies that are developing an online strategy usually put at least the marketing director, computer specialist, financial officer, and CEO online. Remember that in creating a site, your company is presenting itself to the online community. Think about who should have input to that image. The employee with the best computer skills may not be the best person to design the site. Everyone who helps design the site needs to have access to the Web not only while the site is being created but also afterward, for ongoing maintenance. But whether you're opening the Web to one person in the company or a hundred, the first step is selecting an Internet service provider (ISP).

Choosing an ISP

Any ISP can serve corporate customers and can set up accounts for multiple users at a business location, but not all offer the level of service that businesses require in order to use the Web and create a site. The most important thing to ask about is the type of access the ISP offers. The one to avoid is a "shell" account. This is the cheapest, most basic type of access, but Web browsers that show graphics don't normally work with it. Instead, users get to the Web with a text-based browser, like Lynx. (See chapter 2 for an illustration of what a Web page looks like with no graphics—pretty dull.)

To see graphics on the Web, users need to run browser software like Mosaic or Netscape. The types of Internet access that will run those browsers are serial-line interface protocol (SLIP), point-to-point protocol (PPP) or PseudoSLIP, which is a shell account that looks like a SLIP account to the computer. SLIP and PPP accounts usually cost a few dollars more than a shell account, but the easy access to the Web with a graphical browser is worth it. Creating a PseudoSLIP account from a shell account isn't something the service provider will do—it's up to the user. The process requires loading special software that makes the modem connection look like a SLIP account to the browser software. To log onto the Internet and use a Web browser, users first have to run the adapter software to dial up the ISP, then they can run Mosaic, Netscape, or other browsers.

After checking out the access, ask the ISP about its backup plans. If an ISP's computer breaks down, or the phone line connecting the computer to the Internet goes down, or even if the ISP disconnects service briefly for system maintenance, your company won't be able to reach the Internet. More important, if you have a Web site stored on their computer, customers won't be able to reach your Web site. Most ISPs have a backup—another computer in a separate location, multiple phone lines or an emergency phone company contact, or a technical specialist who's always on call in case the system has trouble. Ask how many shut downs have occurred in the past three months, and ask how long it took to bring the system back up each time.

Another area for concern is security. What protection does the ISP have against computer hackers who might try to break into the system and steal credit card numbers or other information? The risk of being hacked is fairly low, but as more consumers begin to use the Internet and make purchases on the Web, and more money begins to flow around online, that risk will increase.

Next, meet the technical people who will be setting up and servicing the account. Who will you call for tech support, and during what hours can you reach them? If there's a time when tech help isn't available, where can you turn if you have a problem? What kind of training is available once the account is hooked up, and does that cost extra? The support staff should be easy to talk to, without tossing around jargony terms.

Don't assume that the ISP will develop or store your Web site. Most do, but some don't, so be sure to ask. Some place size limits on Web sites; others might not handle corporate Web sites, only small ones for their consumer users. Some ISPs handle every step of site development, from design to ongoing maintenance. Others leave all of that responsibility up to the company and only provide computer storage space for the site. Either way can work well for a small company. Make sure that you know what Web services your ISP offers, and that those match your company's needs. (Chapters 4 and 5 give guidelines for deciding which option is best for your company.)

After finding a reliable ISP, the next step is setting up the necessary Internet hardware and software. The bare minimum is a computer with a modem connected to a phone line. Anytime someone wants to use the Internet, they walk over to that computer, dial the ISP with the modem, and log on. The other option is to set up access from any computer on the in-house network. This setup requires hardware that's a bit more advanced, such as a modem pool that anyone on the network can access, or a separate modem for each computer.

Internet access isn't just how companies connect to the Web. If a site is stored on a computer inside your company, it's also how customers get to you. It's important to have a fast phone line connecting that in-house Web site to an Internet backbone node. If you just run a regular phone line, connecting a 28.8 bps modem to your ISP, all of your Web site visitors will slow down once they get jammed into that slow connection, no matter how fast their own connections were up to that point.

To connect to the Internet, all computers use some kind of communications software. It tells the modem where to dial and then connects to the ISP computer when it answers the call. It's possible to access the Internet with just communications and browser software, but then reading email would require a familiarity with UNIX programming language. For those who aren't on intimate terms with UNIX, there are many software packages on the market that make it easier for network and individual Internet access. These packages provide point-and-click graphics for Internet email, discussion groups, file downloading, and browser software for the Web. Any ISP can recommend a software package, or refer to the appendix for several recommended names.

Many ISPs have Internet access software on their computers. Once users connect to the ISP, they type a command that opens up the ISP's email software or Web browser software. The advantage is that the software doesn't use your computer's memory, since it's stored on the ISP's computer. The disadvantage is that sometimes there are too many people using the software at once, and you can't access it.

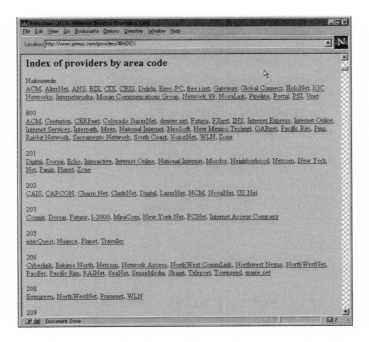

The Web itself is a good place to find resources, such as this site that lists national Internet service providers by area code.

Dialup Access

Remember the early commercial Internet service providers from chapter 1? They're the ones who bought computers in the late 1980s, ran phone lines to Internet nodes (a collection of computers storing Internet information), and started charging customers to access the Internet via modem using their connection. This is option number one: Your modem dials up the ISP and connects to the Internet, thus it's called "dialup" access. By now, many of those early ISPs have grown to become large public companies with a national customer base, like UUNET Technologies and PSINet. Others have stayed small, offering personalized local service, such as Software Tool and Die in Boston and InterAccess in Chicago.

A dialup account for one user can cost as little as twenty dollars per month for unlimited hours of use, or it can cost a few dollars an hour, depending on the service provider. Corporate pricing depends on the number of users and the connection speed. Large national services tend to be more expensive than smaller, local providers, but the larger services also tend to be more reliable, rarely shutting access down because of glitches, upgrades, or repairs. Technical help is often more professional and reliable from large services.

Online Service Access

Another type of dialup Internet service is available from the online services. Many small companies get their feet wet on the Internet by first subscribing to Compu-Serve, Prodigy, or America Online and utilizing their Internet gateways and Web browsers. In addition to Netscape's Navigator, CompuServe offers Spry's version of Mosaic, and Prodigy and America Online have their own browsers.

Setting up this kind of account is easier than working with some ISPs, since the online services offer free easy-to-use software disks. Online service sub-scribers just load the software onto the computer and then run through a series of setup screens to sign up. Technical help comes free with the deal, although it can be tough getting through the ever-busy phone lines. Another attraction is that the online services offer their own information and entertainment along-side the Internet connections and Web browsers. CompuServe is particularly popular because of its financial and business databases (like Dun & Bradstreet reports) that subscribers can browse.

The disadvantage to the online services is that they are more expensive than the twenty-to-thirty-dollar monthly subscription fee than an ISP charges. The services usually charge a flat monthly fee, plus an additional per-hour charge. However, it is easy to find special deals. Each service usually offers one free month or a certain number of free hours to users, so a smart tactic would be to install the software and sign up with one, use the service during the free time period to browse the Web while also researching potential ISPs, and after the free time expires, cancel the service and sign up with the best ISP.

If, however, you're willing to pay more to use an online service and its user-friendly interface, you can design and store a very simple Web site from this type of account. Intended for online service subscribers who want to put up small Web sites, this option doesn't let companies process online sales. But it can be a smart and inexpensive way to test-run a Web site before investing heavily in an online strategy—especially for companies that already subscribe to an online service. (More about this option, and other ways of creating a Web site, in chapter 4.)

CASE STUDY

Copytech: Testing the Internet with Dialup Service

In 1993, Jeff Weener started exploring the Internet with an inexpensive dialup connection to a local ISP. His print company,

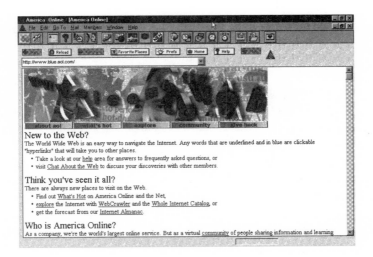

New to the Web?

The World Wide Web is an easy way to navigate the Internet. Any words that are underlined and in blue are clickable "hyperlinks" that will take you to other places.

- Take a look at our help area for answers to frequently asked questions, or
- visit Chat About the Web to discuss your discoveries with other members.

Think you've seen it all?

There are always new places to visit on the Web.

- Find out What's Hot on America Online and the Net,
- explore the Internet with WebCrawler and the Whole Internet Catalog, or
- get the forecast from our Internet Almanac.

Who is America Online?

As a company, we're the world's largest online service. But as a virtual community of people sharing information and learning

Commercial online services offer Internet access and their own Web browser software.

Copytech, does documentation for high-tech companies, and when customers started going online, Weener knew he had to follow. "I started seeing email addresses on people's business cards," he says. "I didn't know anything about the Internet. It was a gamble for us to get an Internet account, a hunch that customers might want to send stuff to us this way. You can't buy an expensive leased line on a hunch, but I was willing to take a risk on dialup service."

The risk quickly paid off, even though Weener didn't set up a Web site right away. He did invest about $350 per month for Internet service. He says his salespeople almost immediately started getting appointments they wouldn't have gotten otherwise. "When we started, it was a major competitive advantage in our industry. Now it's a necessity of doing business." In a few weeks, having Internet access won the company new customers, who sent jobs directly to Copytech's email address, saving time and money in mailing or courier delivery.

The $12 million company upgraded to a leased line in 1995, when about a dozen of the top customers were consistently sending their work via the Internet. "They wanted a faster connection," Weener says. "People were sending files so large that it would take hours to download." It was a $10,000 increase in service, but it was worth it. "Having this high-tech capability excites people." It also enabled Weener to finally set up a Web site, which debuted in July 1995.

Dialup service is the least expensive type of Internet access. It's also the slowest, because it's based on the speed of the modem used to connect to the ISP. A 38,400 bits per second modem is one of the fastest currently available, but it still takes several seconds to "load" (find and display) an average Web site. That may not seem like a long time, but multiply it by the many sites that you load each time you browse the Web, and it gets pretty tedious. As three-dimensional browsers become more popular, it takes far longer to download the sites designed for them. For serious browsing, two types of higher-speed Web access are available from the local phone company or ISP.

Leased Line Access

A leased line is a phone line that runs from a company to an ISP, and it carries data only between those two sites. It gives the company a SLIP or PPP account for connecting to the Internet. Called a dedicated line because it's dedicated to that one function—moving data between two fixed points—this type of phone line can't be used for anything else. Leased, or dedicated, lines are commonly called "pipelines" or more simply, "pipes."

The capacity of leased phone lines can be described several ways. Some people refer to it as "size," because each type of line can hold only a specific amount of data at any given moment. Others refer to the capacity as "speed," because each phone line moves that data along at a different speed. The correct technical term to describe both speed and size is "bandwidth," though these terms are used pretty much interchangeably. The smallest, or slowest, leased line available is 56K, which moves data along at 56,000 bits per second (compared to the 28,800 bits per second speed of a 28.8 baud modem). The next step up is a T1 line, which moves data at 1.544 million bits per second. The fastest line currently available is a T3 line, whizzing data along at 45 million bits per second.

Think of it this way: A two-megabyte document (roughly the size of a thirty-page Web site with several color graphics) will take about twelve minutes to download on a 28.8 baud modem, six minutes on a 56K line, fifteen seconds on a T1 line, and half a second on a T3 line. Assuming that the phone line is connected to a computer server that can handle the traffic, a 56K line might hold about one hundred visitors to a Web site at one time. A T1 can handle several thousand simultaneous connections, and a T3 can take tens of thousands. Most of the phone lines connecting the core Internet backbone sites to each other are T1 and T3 lines.

T1 and T3 lines are fast but expensive. Many companies choose instead to lease a "fractional" T1 line: The line connecting their company to an Internet backbone node is a T1, but they pay only for the part of the phone line they actually use at any given moment. Although the line may hold, say, a total of three thousand visitors logged on at the same time, the company pays only for the actual number on the phone line, not the full capacity. Two, three, or more companies may be sharing the same fractional T1 line. If one experiences a sudden boom in traffic, the others may have problems allowing access to the site. Some ISPs, however, dedicate one leased line per company. So even though the client may only use and pay for part of the T1 line, they have the entire line available at all times in case they need it.

An increasingly popular type of leased line is a "frame-relay" connection, which is available only in some parts of the country and only in speeds slower than T1. Companies using frame-relay service usually pay less than for a leased line of the same speed. The costs of leased line service varies across the country. For a 56K, expect to pay around $500 per month. A T1 line ranges from $1,000 to several thousand dollars per month, depending on whether the company has full or fractional service. A T3 runs from several thousand to tens of thousands of dollars per month.

Leased lines are available from the phone company. If your Web site is stored at an ISP, they will probably already have package pricing for full and fractional leased lines and will usually be responsible for servicing those lines if they go down. (More on the services involved in outsourcing Web sites and phone line options in chapter 5.) If your Web site is stored in-house (see chapter 4), you'll have to purchase the line yourself. Most companies then hire their ISP to service the phone lines and make sure they're always up and running.

CASE STUDY

Aleph: Leasing a Dedicated Phone Line

Michael Demetrius has had his leased line since 1994. His startup translation service company, Aleph, is based in San Francisco and Demetrius stores the site on an in-house Macintosh computer. For translators and customers to exchange files any time of the day or night, Demetrius needed a dedicated phone line. In 1994, the fastest he could get was 14.4 bps, for $200 per month. "Obviously everyone always wants more speed," he says. "But at that time browsers weren't as sophisticated, so we kept our pages simple and speed wasn't a problem."

Demetrius upgraded a year later to 128 bps, as part of a fractional T1 line rather than buying the whole line. He admits that not owning the entire pipeline can sometimes cause traffic backup problems because most ISPs buy a T1 line, then sell more than T1 capacity for that line. When buying a fractional line, he advises selecting an ISP who has the capacity you need right now, "Don't buy your connection on a promise of there being new lines in the future—there are a lot of promises made that don't get met." Despite the backups, Demetrius claims that his translators and clients have never had trouble accessing the site to pick up or drop off manuscripts. That's partly because most of them are using email to exchange files, and since email waits until the pipe is free, it doesn't matter how busy it is during peak times. "Since we're not really about fancy graphics and video files, we don't need the full T1."

The cost for his faster connection is $200 per month, the same as the early 14.4 bps. That's because Demetrius gets the faster phone line from a smaller ISP. "In the early days, you were forced to go with one of the big guys," he says. He relied on BBN, which provided reliable but expensive service. With the birth of smaller ISPs, Demetrius changed to one in the same building as Aleph. "That way we don't pay phone bills to connect to them, and that's half the connection costs." He estimates that the same line speed would cost about $600 from BBN.

Service from a smaller provider is not as reliable, he admits. "It's been down. Problem with going with smaller guys is you're farther off the main trunk of the Internet, so when errors happen it's not necessarily our ISP. They're buying from someone else, who's buying from someone who's buying from AT&T. It means that the odds of the line going down are greater because we're more hops away. Once every three to four months the line goes down for a few hours."

For companies that are shopping for a leased line, Demetrius advises getting a connection that's simple and slow until you know you need more. "Start at 28.8 bps and see how that goes. If users start complaining or you're refusing connections to some users, then it's time to up to 56K. ISPs will work with you, and they won't charge fees for upping speed. A lot of people go straight for a T1, but that's overkill at first."

ISDN Access

The other type of high-speed Internet connection is via an integrated services digital network (ISDN) phone line, a specific type of digital phone line available from the local phone company. ISDN lines can carry voice and data over the same cable. Each channel moves that data along at 64,000 bits per second, and the two channels can be combined for one super-fast channel at 128,000 bits per second—about four times faster than a 28.8 modem. With an ISDN, a business can have a fax machine transmission or an online connection as well as a voice conversation running over the same phone line simultaneously.

It sounds like a great service, but there are several reasons why only about 300,000 users had signed up for ISDN in the United States by early 1996. The first problem is that it costs more than a regular phone line. Although hooking up to ISDN service usually involves merely throwing a switch at the phone company, the fee for that can be several hundred dollars. In addition to a monthly fee for voice and data calls, some phone companies add a per-minute charge for data calls. Lower-priced incentive packages exist for small business and home users, but business service still varies widely by region, anywhere from about $30 to $100 per month.

Also, ISDN lines don't work with standard modems. Companies must install several small hardware boxes, including a "terminal adapter," which translates all phone and computer signals going out of the office into ISDN signals, and an "NT1," which splits the existing phone line into the separate ISDN channels. This equipment, available separately or bundled together, is sometimes called a "digital modem."

The second reason that ISDN service isn't more popular is that it's still difficult to reach the Web with ISDN. It gives users a SLIP or PPP connection so

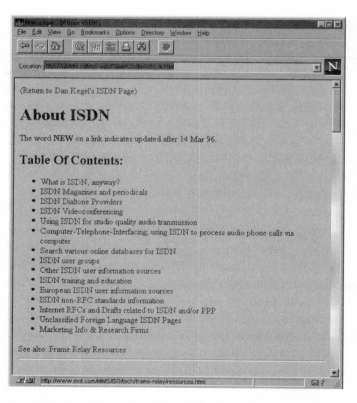

Everything there is to know about ISDN phone service—and other kinds of Internet connectivity—is available on the Web.

that they can use Web browsers like Mosaic or Netscape, but very few ISPs are equipped to handle an ISDN connection. The ISPs that do support ISDN often charge up to three times more than the per-hour connection fee for a regular dialup connection. But because the connection moves more quickly, the benefit may be worth the cost.

The third problem is availability. Not every phone company offers ISDN, and of the ones that do, many don't advertise the fact. Customers who call asking about ISDN service are frequently brushed off by salespeople who aren't familiar with the service. Where ISDN isn't available, there might be a service called "virtual ISDN" or "alternate-served ISDN." Basically, the service is available, but from a phone company switching station that's farther away from the one get that provides your normal phone service.

CASE STUDY

Lab-Beta: Relying on ISDN

Don Roudebush's startup software-testing company relies heavily on ISDN service. He first learned about the service while working for an ISDN equipment manufacturer and has been a convert ever since. He's been using it in his Simi Valley, California, office since starting his company, Lab-Beta, in the fall of 1995.

"I test huge programs," he says. "I get most of my source code via the Internet, and if I got it with a 28.8 baud modem, I'd be online all night." Roudebush pays about $150 per month for ISDN service from his Internet provider. "It's great on the Web," he says. "I don't have to go to sleep while I'm connecting to a graphics-intensive site and then wake up to see what it looks like."

To get the service, Roudebush signed a two-year contract with Pacific Bell, who waived the $100 installation fee. Local phone service is $30 per month, plus per-minute charges. "I'm kind of a brand-name person," he says of his top-end equipment. He bought an AT&T NT1 box for just under $300. His router, Ascend's Pipeline 50MX, was $1,500.

As with any phone installation, the phone company leaves inside wiring up to the customer. Because Roudebush was very familiar with ISDN equipment and how the service works, he installed the hardware himself. But it's not like setting up a computer, which almost anyone can do without professional help. "I would recommend spending the few dollars it costs to have someone come in and do the work," he says. "It will only take a few hours. If you don't know what you're doing, it could take you weeks."

Why did Roudebush buy ISDN and not a leased line? Cost and control, he says. "A leased line is only point-to-point connectivity, so I could only connect to a single customer. With ISDN I can call anyone." He also didn't want to buy the extra hardware that a leased line requires, or pay the higher monthly charges. "A T1 line would have cost me $350 per month," he says. "As a small business, I couldn't justify that cost."

One scary thing about an Internet connection is that as long as you can get *out* to connect to other computers, other people can use those same lines to get *in* to your company. This is a good thing, if you have an in-house Web site or computer bulletin board service that you want customers or vendors to reach; they can dial up your computer and look at what you store there—product, company, or technical help information. But it's not good when someone reaches computers that store sensitive information, such as invoices, purchase orders, or customer records.

Firewall Protection

Whether your company has a dialup connection or a dedicated line, experienced computer users can "hack," or break into, any computers that are connected to the modem line. If your company network is connected to the computers that also access the Internet, this can be a scary risk. One recent Ernst & Young survey of 1,290 companies found that one out of every five companies had been hacked via their Internet connection during the past year. The Computer Emergency Response Team, associated with Carnegie Mellon University, handled 2,412 Internet-related security incidents during 1995— almost double the number they recorded for 1993. Most hackers aren't actually interested in your valuable business information. They just want to shut down a site and then brag about it to their friends. Although your data isn't really worth anything to them, you do lose time repairing the system, and you lose potential customers who can't get to the site when it's closed. Small businesses are particularly vulnerable to hacking because they rarely bother to invest in firewall protection. Hackers know this.

To protect against being hacked, many companies put in "firewalls," or software and hardware systems designed to deter hackers. Who needs firewalls? Anyone with a modem line that connects in-house computers to a remote location is at risk for being hacked. Companies need to consider how large that risk is. Is the modem line open all the time (a leased line) or just periodically to receive and send email? A company that only has dialup Internet access is at a much lower risk of being hacked, because the modem line is only connecting periodically to the Internet. A leased line is a greater risk, because it's always connected.

The most basic, cheapest, and safest type of protection isn't actually a firewall, but a hardware setup known as "airgapping." It's as simple as making sure the computer or computers connected to the Internet aren't also connected to any other in-house computers, and don't store any sensitive information on those Internet computers. A hacker can still get to your Web site and change or crash that. But since there's no physical connection to the network, there's no way a hacker can get to your internal computers from the Web site. It's the only solution that absolutely protects the network computers.

A firewall is software that sits on a computer somewhere between the network computers and the computer that connects to the Internet. So although the Internet computer is connected to the network, there's a little software wall between the two through which all messages and files and users must pass. It acts as a guard, halting all traffic between the network and the Internet computer and asking for identification. Any person or data without the proper identification or password gets turned away. With the password, people and data can get into the company's network or out of the network and on to the Web.

There are three types of firewalls—packet filter, circuit level, and application gateway. Using these software programs, a systems administrator programs the firewall to let certain kinds of computer users in and out. This requires frequent updating of the software, adding and subtracting criteria for entry. Sometimes firewalls can be cracked if the hacker figures out the codes to allow his or her computer into the system—basically figuring out a fake password that tricks the guard. The application gateway type is the most expensive and the most secure, as it has a higher level of tests that can be programmed for accepting and denying access. Packet filter is the simplest and cheapest, starting at a few thousand dollars, and circuit level falls somewhere between the two. Firewall software can sit on the same computer as the Internet connection or it can be on a separate computer altogether.

In addition to tracking access in and out of the company, firewall software also prints out logs of this activity. The system administrator can read through these activity logs to see who is going in and out through the Internet connection. If someone is repeatedly trying to come in using different passwords, the system administrator would notice that suspicious activity and could program the system to keep that person out.

CASE STUDY

Bluestone Consulting: Buying a Firewall

Bluestone Consulting, a software development company, knew it needed firewall protection when it first connected to a 56K line for Internet service in early 1995. "It's not like we're doing Department of Defense work," says Doug Miller, manager of information systems at the $16 million company. "But I had to determine a worst-case scenario if someone we didn't want came in. We have a fiduciary duty to protect personnel data. There's client information that someone could use to jeopardize our market position, and development efforts that could be used to jeopardize our product and sales departments. If someone hacked into our internal router just for kicks, we'd have lost work, and that's really a big issue. If we lose a directory, that's lost time to rebuild it."

Miller spent six months researching firewalls while Bluestone worked on setting up the company Web site, which they store on an in-house computer. During that time, Miller surfed the Internet for information on firewalls. He also read *Firewalls and Internet Security: Repelling the Wiley Hacker* (Bill Cheswick and Steve Bellovin, Addison-Wesley, 1994), which he calls the industry bible for Internet security. Based on his research, he decided on a hardware/software package called the Gauntlet Internet Firewall System, from Trusted Information Systems.

Although TIS makes a version of their firewall software available as shareware (called FireWall Tool Kit) to download off the Internet, Miller chose to pay $15,000 for the commercial version and full installation, plus another $1,000 per month for upgrades and support. He chose that version because the share-ware wasn't being upgraded regularly by TIS—it was an early version of the software, complete with bugs and without the patches and fixes of later upgrades. Miller and the other Blue-stone techies are pretty comfortable with software and at one point even considered configuring their own firewall software, but they decided that it would take too much labor to set up and maintain. Buying a package that came with regular upgrade service was a more cost-effective option.

The software gives Miller an hourly report of any suspicious activity, as well as a daily report of all activity over the modem line, including unsuccessful attempts. He spends only about an hour a week maintaining the firewall, mostly adding and removing new and old employees from the user database and backing up the data so it can be re-installed in case it crashes.

Bluestone runs the firewall software on a separate machine from the Web site because everything going through their modem—email, Web traffic, employees modeming out to reach the Internet—goes through the firewall first. "It's worth the money to buy a separate machine just for the firewall software," Miller says. "You don't want to allocate processing power on the firewall computer to Web functions, because that will slow down everything else—like email—going through the fire-wall." They chose a Pentium/60, running a version of UNIX called BSD version 2.0; both the hardware and software were included in the firewall package price.

So far, one would-be hacker tried thirty-five times in a row to log in using an unauthorized password. Another time, Miller noticed on his firewall log reports repeated failed attempts to get into his system through every online service the company runs—email and several file downloading functions. Both times, the firewall held.

Who Should Be Online?

Many companies limit Web access to the few key employees working directly on the Web site because they worry about lost productivity. The cheapest way to control access is simply to leave modems off the computers of employees who don't need to be online. A company with one or two dedicated Internet connection computers in a central location can offer access to everyone in the company, and at the same time easily monitor who's using the connection and for how long.

Losing production time while employees browse the latest hip page or chat with overseas friends via email is the main reason companies limit access. Another reason is the overlap between personal and professional use of the Internet. If an employee sends email from the company Internet account, the company name and address are automatically attached to that email message. If that message is less than professional, it can reflect badly on the company. It can also make the company legally responsible for any questionable Internet activity on the part of employees. All companies with Internet access—even if that's just email—should have a written online policy in the company employee handbook. That policy should spell out what is considered appropriate online behavior and what steps the company will take to ensure that the behavior is followed. Some companies even monitor employee email. The issue of whether the company or employee owns an employee's email is still being decided in the courts, but the weight is heavily in the company's favor.

But cutting off all Internet use isn't the only solution. Some companies limit the areas that employees can go to, cutting off access to all "X-rated" Web sites, for example. Some companies allow full access to all parts of the Web and Internet but monitor what employees are browsing and address improper usage problems as they arise. They do this with software that lets a network administrator block access to specific sites or types of sites or lets the administrator see what sites employees are visiting. Some firewall software will also control access in another way: Instead of programming which sites aren't available, the system administrator programs which sites employees *can* access.

CASE STUDY

Park City Group: Limiting Employee Access

Instead of asking himself why employee access to the Web should be limited, Randy Fields asked himself why his employees should have Web access at all. "I couldn't find any reason that all of our employees needed to spend a lot of time there. What technical resources we need you can find in an Internet news-group in ten minutes," he says. So the CEO of Park City Group, a Park City, Utah–based software company, doesn't give Web access to employees unless they specifically ask for it. "If they need it for business reasons, we'll do that." Instead, everyone has email accounts and access to other sections of the Internet.

For employees who do need to use the Web, and for access to the company's own Web site, Fields has set up one machine that's isolated from the rest of the network. Not only is it an inexpensive firewall solution, but it limits personal browsing for his 130 employees. "When you're sitting at the Web machine, you're in plain view," he says. "There's a self-discipline associated with it, so people don't misuse the resource."

Once you've gotten an Internet account with Web access and you've spent a little time looking around, it's time to think about setting up your own company's Web site. One of the most exciting things about the Web is that anyone can quickly learn how to navigate and how to set up a site. It's much easier to understand how to put together the elements of a Web site than, say, how to rewrite DOS files on a computer. And because it's so easy, many companies design and maintain their own Web sites without a lot of in-house technical expertise. There are several options for creating, storing, and maintaining the site, whether it's done entirely in-house, completely outsourced, or some combination of the two. The next few chapters explore those options.

4

●●●●●●●●●●●●●●●●●●●●●●●●

Quality Control: Building Your Site In-House

Developing a Web site has two stages: Building the initial site, and making ongoing changes while maintaining it. In the building phase, a company (perhaps working with a Web designer or developer) plans and creates how the site will look. The company also writes software for the site's different processes, such as making sales or receiving customer email. In the maintenance phase, usually called "serving," the site is stored on either the company's or a service provider's computer. On a regular basis, someone gathers the customer email and responds to it. Someone processes the online sales and fills orders. Someone makes changes to the site, updating the company data, product or service listings, and prices. And someone makes sure the site's computer and phone line are always working correctly.

There are three ways to build and serve a Web site. In the first, serving in-house, the site is built and served entirely within the company, by employees using in-house computer hardware and software. This option offers the most control over the product because companies can design whatever they like and make changes whenever they like. It's usually faster to set up because all decisions are made in-house, without involving an extra level of outside consultants. This option is also the most expensive, because the company pays for all labor, computer hardware and software, and a dedicated line.

In the second approach, both development and maintenance are outsourced entirely to professionals. This option, less expensive than the in-house site, usually results in the best-looking sites. After all, what small company keeps an experienced Web site designer on staff? Hiring a consultant who develops sites full time frees the company to focus on its core competency. Outsourcing the site maintenance to a full-time server company offers the assurance of computer professionals who are dedicated to keeping the site accessible twenty-four hours a day. The server company will also process secure online sales transactions, forward customer email gathered at the site, and provide tracking statistics regarding visitor traffic.

The disadvantages to an outsourced site are that it can be time-consuming to develop, because designers and company representatives often sit through meeting after meeting during the building phase; the finished product is only as good as the designer, and choosing one who will stay in business and create a site that accurately reflects the sensibility of a company can be difficult; and storing the site at a server company scares some small businesses, who don't want their Web sites on the same computers as other sites, for various security reasons. (Outsourced sites are covered in chapter 5.)

The last option is a hybrid of in-house development and outsourcing, and it's the cheapest solution of all. The building phase is handled in-house, but once it's finished, the site is stored at an outside ISP for serving. The company doesn't outsource the content updates, only the technical support and maintenance. Someone at the company regularly checks the site and makes all changes, gathers email, and processes sales (if the site offers them). Cost-conscious companies can easily design and build Web sites in-house, frequently learning as they go. The site is usually stored with an inexpensive ISP, often the same one that provides their company or personal email service. Often, limited Web site storage is included in an ISP's monthly fee. (More on the hybrid approach in chapter 5.)

CASE STUDY

Oak Ridge Public Relations: Serving a Site In-House

Oak Ridge Public Relations, a Cupertino, California–based public relations firm, put up a Web site in early 1995. From the very beginning, vice president Tom Keenan knew he would build and serve the site in-house. His ISP advised him to create a hybrid site, storing the site with them and handling the content updates himself. But Keenan decided it wasn't right for him, even though his $880,000 company is smaller than most that make that decision.

"I didn't see the site as an end in itself," Keenan explains. "It seems like there's more to be done with the Internet than just a Web site. And the more control I have over the facilities, the more likely I am to be able to take advantage of those things. It's forced me to learn a lot more about the Internet and what we can do with it." Already, Oak Ridge is experimenting with electronic mailing lists and online discussion groups. And Keenan already credits the site with earning him two clients and a steady stream of prospects.

Keenan built the site himself. In order to get the site up quickly while he was away on a business trip, he chose consultants to begin designing the site based on his preliminary plans. Keenan admits that finding a reliable Web developer can be difficult. "Everyone's hanging up a shingle and saying they do it," he says. "And some are good. You have to look at what they've done and get referrals. Ask the referrals, Were they on time? Did they come up with interesting ideas? What would you do differently now if you started all over with them again?"

After he returned from his trip, Keenan took over building the site. "Web design is not brain surgery," he says. "I started out with the basic design of what we wanted and explained that to the consultants. Then I took it over and now I do all the updates myself." From the Web, he downloaded "freeware," or free software, called Webserver and still uses that to maintain the site. That might change, he says. "I suspect we'll shift over to a commercial server like Netscape for the assurance of continued technical support."

Oak Ridge uses a Macintosh computer network. But at the time he was setting up his Web site, Keenan couldn't find any Web server software for Macs, so he bought a Sun SPARCstation Five computer to store the Web site. "I probably could have saved a lot of money if I'd gone with a [PC] clone," he says. "But my experience with clones hasn't been great." He chose UNIX over Windows software because he felt it was more reliable. "Basically I wanted to get equipment that I wouldn't have to worry about for five years." The total hardware costs were about $15,000 after Keenan added a few disks to expand his computer's memory.

For his connection to the Internet, Keenan has a dedicated 56K leased line from Pacific Bell, which cost $1,500 to install, plus $100 per month for service. Keenan is already thinking of upgrading to a much faster T1 line through his ISP, BBN Planet in Cambridge, Massachusetts.

For security, Oak Ridge has a nonproprietary firewall installation from BreakAway Technologies that uses standard UNIX network protection setups. "If we had a UNIX network in the rest of the company, there would be real protection issues," says Keenan. Because most computer programmers are familiar with the workings of UNIX hardware and pro-gramming, it can be fairly easy to hack a UNIX network. "But all the rest of our machines are Macs, and there are some real substantial difficulties in hacking that." Just to double-check, Keenan asked his brother-in-law, a computer programmer, to try to reach his network through the UNIX Web server com-puter. He failed.

The biggest advantage to in-house serving is also the biggest disadvantage, Keenan says. "I have complete responsi-bility. If I don't have enough space, I can buy a disk and put it on my computer. If my ISP didn't have enough space, I'd have to wait for him to upgrade." Last December a storm knocked out Oak Ridge's power for twenty-four hours, and Keenan quickly learned about the flip side of that responsibility. "Our site was down, and I had to deal with it instead of relying on someone else. But that was a freak occurrence—if the site had been stored somewhere else here, they'd be out of power too. The worst thing that could happen is the office could burn down. But then I'd have more than the Web site to worry about."

Who Should Serve a Web Site In-House?

Setting up an in-house site is easiest and cheapest for companies that already have expertise and hardware to spare. For this reason, few small retailers serve their own Web sites, but many high-tech companies do. Here's a checklist to help decide whether or not your company should develop its site in-house. If your company can identify with two or more of these statements, in-house serving is probably better than outsourcing.

We've got the best computer geeks in the industry working here: Labor is the largest expense of creating and maintaining a successful Web site, and the make-or-break factor in deciding whether or not to keep the site in-house. A consultant may already know the Web but has to learn about your company. Companies with in-house technical people have a big advantage in that those employees already know the company culture, strategy, and core competency. And if they're not already familiar with Internet technology, they can learn that more quickly than a consultant can learn your company's inner workings. Bear in mind that someone has to be following the One-Hour Browse Rule and then making ongoing changes to keep the site exciting.

We rely heavily on a sophisticated phone system: Running a site in-house requires keeping one phone line continually open so visitors can access the site. Many telemarketing companies, for example, already lease dedicated phone lines, one of which can be used for connecting to the Internet. The cost for a leased line is fairly affordable, as low as $500 per month (see chapter 3), so a company with computers to spare and in-house expertise should consider investing in a leased line. If it's the only piece missing from the puzzle, it's more cost-effective to buy the line and save on labor rather than farming out the whole site.

We've got someone always on call in case the computers go down: This is what a large part of the monthly fee to a server company pays for. Once the site opens, someone will always have to be on call in case the Web site computer develops a glitch and visitors can't reach it. Or in case the phone lines go down. Or in case someone hacks the system and breaks into the network. The risk of hacking is still fairly rare, and sites and phone lines don't shut down all that frequently, but a contingency plan is essential in case it happens. If your company already has a disaster strategy in place, with someone on call twenty-four hours a day, why hire a company to maintain the Web connection? Add it to the disaster recovery plan. If it goes down, a company person is on call to handle it.

We've got a pretty computer-intensive business: Moving an outdated 386 or 486 PC computer to Web duty isn't even an expense. Purchasing one is a minor line-item expense for a company that regularly spends for technology.

We want to link our Web site to our in-house product database: This isn't easy for companies that want to outsource the site, because the database is in one location and the Web site is in another. To link the site to any kind of in-house database that will update listings and process transactions, companies have to run a high-speed modem line connecting the database to the Web site. Visitors browsing the Web site can then access the most current information. If a database is a major part of your company's Web site, you might as well serve it in-house.

We are completely committed to a Web strategy for the next few years: Many companies are still getting their feet wet, not sure that the Web is a viable commercial outlet. They want to test drive a site and see what happens. But if your company is already convinced that the Web is the future, and management is itching to test the possibilities, then serving the site in-house offers fuller Internet access for better learning about the new medium.

If, after taking this brief quiz, your company decides that outsourcing is more cost-effective, don't rule out eventually bringing the site in-house. Many companies begin by outsourcing, then later move the site inside. Companies that might want to do this in the future should bear that in mind when signing a contract with designers and ISPs. Otherwise, someone else could end up owning part of your company's site, and you can't take it with you when you move. (More on this and other legal issues in chapter 5.)

CASE STUDY

Univenture: Moving an Outsourced Site In-House

"Even if our site didn't take off, we knew we'd eventually want to bring it in-house," says Ross Youngs of Univenture. This CD-packaging manufacturer originally outsourced their Web site in the fall of 1994 because they arranged a deal with a local government funded project. "It seemed like a logical way to jump into it," he says. "We only had to pay for production and we were online." North American Trade Point in Columbus,

Ohio, served the site at their location without charging Univenture monthly storage fees.

After the site had been up for six months, the $12 million company brought the site in-house. "Luckily, we're a large enough company that we could afford to have someone take a good hard look at what kind of setup we needed," Youngs says. "Our in-house guy purchased most of the hardware, with advice from consultants." The consultants charged about $1,000 to evaluate Univenture's hardware and software needs. Univenture now serves their Web site from a Pentium 120 with 32 megabytes of RAM; it runs Windows NT and is connected to a 56K leased line.

For companies thinking of one day bringing an outsourced site in-house, Youngs advises telling the ISP up front that you might take that route. Make sure to secure a commitment stating that they're prepared to help make that transition later.

Equipment Fundamentals

Once a company decides to bring a site in-house—whether for initial development or after it's been outsourced for a while—there's certain equipment that every site needs. A wide range of hardware and software is available, in a wide range of prices. Some companies invest in name brands, others work with free software and older-model computers. Remember, it's always easier to start small and upgrade later.

Hardware

Running a Web site requires a computer dedicated just to storing the site. The type of computer will dictate how long it takes Web users to download your site. It's better if this computer doesn't have anything else on it, even the company's Internet email software—it will only slow the download time.

A 486 PC or PowerMac is the minimum computer that will work, with as much random access memory, or RAM, that the company can afford, hopefully at least 12 megabytes. The more RAM the computer has, the faster the site loads for visitors. A complicated, graphic-intensive site will need more RAM than a small, mostly-text site. The minimum that developers recommend is 16 megabytes. The computer's hard drive should be at least one gigabyte to have storage room for graphics.

Using a system this stripped-down is risky. When visitors try to access a Web site that's too full to accommodate them, they get an error message saying that the server can't be found; many users won't try to return a second time. This system also leaves little room for growth, so if the Web site suddenly becomes very popular, expect the site to load very slowly for visitors and probably crash and shut down often. And upgrading the system will require buying new hardware instead of simply expanding the existing system. As design software like Java becomes more popular, lots of the memory-intensive activities on a Web site will be performed by the visitor's computer, so the site host computer won't need huge amounts of processing power.

The more large graphics a site has, or if it is performing real-time activities like showing a current photo of the view from outside the company offices, the more processing power the host computer will need—at least a Pentium 100. A tip from those who've been hardware shopping: Check out the lower prices of used equipment.

Software

To store sites, computers need an operating system (OS), such as Windows NT or DOS, plus Web server software and site design software. The cheapest option is to download all this as free software from the Internet, but companies must balance this against the possible labor cost of having someone learn new software. (Not everyone knows how to use the free UNIX-based operating system LINUX, for example). The OS must have multitasking capabilities—the power to perform several tasks at once; Windows NT, UNIX, Apple System 7, and IBM OS/2 all do. With multitasking, several visitors can connect and access information simultaneously, while the system processes data in the background (like updating a product database).

Phone Line

The most that the bare-bones hardware setup outlined above could handle is a T1 leased line, and only if that weren't filled to capacity with people visiting the site at the same time. A good bet is to try a 56K line, fractional T1 service, or a plain old modem line until it's clear what the response to your site is. For companies considering leased line service, contact the phone company early—some have waiting lists. Some companies have been forced to postpone opening their Web sites because their leased line installation was later than they had originally planned. (For more about phone lines, see Chapter 3.)

Firewall

The cheapest—and most foolproof—solution to preventing hackers from breaking into the company network is to keep the Web computer physically separated from all other computers in the office. Don't network it, and don't run a modem line to it. This will protect the network as long as the company isn't also running outside email or other Internet access on another computer connected to a leased phone line somewhere else in the company. Remember that any modem line running from the network to the world at large is a risk, whether it's open all the time or not. If the Web site is supposed to be connected to the network in some way, such as to an in-house database, consider one of the available firewall software packages. Remember that the more interactive the Web site—forms to fill out and send in, company information to browse, and email responses—the more openings for hackers to get in.

Domain Name

For a computer to be recognized by the rest of the Internet, it must be registered. Every computer connected to the Internet has a number, like "192.322.11.74.54," registered by the service provider to which that computer is connected. But attaching a name to that number makes it easier for everyone on the Internet to remember, including the company that owns it. So a computer with a number becomes "mycompany.com." That means the company email goes to "me@mycompany.com" and your Web site is at "www.mycompany.com." To secure this computer name, or "domain," the company must register it with Inter-NIC, a nonprofit organization formed to handle registrations. In 1996, registration cost $100 for two years, then $50 per year after that. (To register, any company can contact InterNIC at their Web site at rs.internic.net/rs-internic.html and follow the onscreen registration process.)

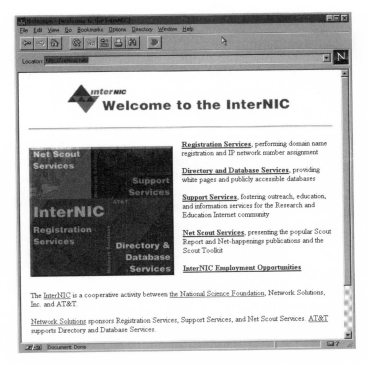

InterNIC's Web site offers online registration for companies that want to secure specific domain names.

It's important to register a domain early in your company's online strategy process. The main reason is because once a company or person registers a domain, nobody else can use it, and "mycompany.com" may already be taken. Few companies get their first choice of domains anymore, so it's smart to draw up a list of viable options before applying to InterNIC. Once the application is made, it can take up to a month for a response—because by 1996, InterNIC was already processing more than a request a minute. (For more information on securing a domain name, see chapter 7.)

Choosing Software

Which OS should a company use to serve their Web site? It's the same debate as which to choose for the network computers, and it's not necessary to choose the same system that runs the rest of the company's computers. A company is making a long-term investment by choosing an OS; the most popular options for Web serving are UNIX, Windows NT, or Macintosh. All Web development software must be compatible, and once a system is configured to work with a particular OS, it's expensive to change. Add to it the cost of updating all the software linked to it, and retraining the people who use it.

People have strong opinions about which OS is best. UNIX users swear by UNIX. Macintosh lovers won't use anything but Macintosh. Windows devotees buy Windows NT. They all work and work well. Choosing one depends on what options are the most important for each individual company. Each OS has some strong advantages and disadvantages for Web use.

UNIX

UNIX is the programming language with which the Internet was built, and the majority of all Web servers remain UNIX computers. Therefore, most people assume that UNIX is the required platform for setting up a Web site. It's certainly the cheapest—many Web freeware and shareware programs written for UNIX are widely available on the Internet itself. Because the OS has been around for years, these programs are pretty well-established, with most of the bugs worked out. The OS itself is available for free on the Internet, as a version called LINUX. UNIX, still the best-known programming language among computer specialists, also offers true multitasking capability, which is essential in a Web server. It is the OS of choice for the powerful Sun computers that many ISPs use for Internet service. A new version of UNIX, called CDE, works on Windows machines.

On the other hand, UNIX is a pretty strange language. Even people who know their way around DOS commands will have trouble figuring it out—commands like "ls" for a directory listing aren't very intuitive. Some users warn that it's difficult to install and takes a lot of attention while running. Many companies that use it employ a full-time administrator to stay on top of it.

For a UNIX-based system, expect to pay about $2,000 for a 486DX computer with 32 megabytes of RAM and a two-gigabyte hard drive. A top-of-the-line Sun SPARCstation or DEC Alpha station system costs from $5,000 to $12,000; add about $50 for a CD-ROM version of the operating system. Web programming software is available free on the Internet (see the appendix for names and where to find it).

CASE STUDY

Advanced Hardware Architecture: Choosing UNIX

"Our Web site would have been up a long time ago," says network administrator Todd Nybo. "But I had to prove to management that it was a useful tool." In 1995, Advanced Hardware Architecture, a $14 million semiconductor manufacturer, already had an Internet email account but hadn't been using the Web. Nybo decided to create a site first, then show it—and the company's competitors' sites—to managers. "I was doing this on my own," he says. "So I wanted to do it without buying anything." Free UNIX software installed on a spare computer was the answer. Setting up the Web site cost Advanced Hardware only about two weeks of Nybo's labor.

Nybo rescued an old 386 PC computer from the company and connected it to the 56K leased line the company already used for email. (The Pullman, Washington–based company paid PSINet $15,000 for the leased line in 1996.) Nybo downloaded LINUX, the free software version of UNIX's operating system, off the Internet. "Not everyone can do it," he admits. "With Windows, you're buying a canned package that's easier to install, and you have technical support." Although experienced programmers regularly exchange email online to share their solutions to UNIX problems, there's no centralized manufacturer support for it. LINUX is a very powerful 32-bit operating system with built-in networking capability, and it does require some programming expertise to set up. "But there are more books on the subject now," Nybo says.

Then he downloaded CERN-HTTPD version 3.0, a free version of hypertext transfer protocol (HTTP) Web development software. He programmed the Web site himself. "It was pretty easy to learn," he says. The twenty-six-page site was up and running in two months; most of that time was spent securing approval for the design from the marketing department. Nybo himself spent two days to get the LINUX and HTTP software installed and running, and another three days were spent designing the site. When the site went live, company management was impressed. "Before, a lot of people were naive about the Web," Nybo says. "Now they tell me to hurry up and update our site."

Windows

Although it's possible to serve a Web site using Windows 95, it doesn't offer as many options as Windows NT. Compared to UNIX, the menu-driven graphical interface makes Windows NT easy to use and easy to install. It's not necessary to pay a programming guru a fat salary to maintain it, because almost anyone can run it. And there's plenty of Windows-compatible software available. NT devotees are betting that available software is likely to tip in Windows' direction in the future, eventually making UNIX obsolete.

The main drawback to running NT is the software cost. The OS itself is expensive, as are all of the programs that run on it, although Microsoft now bundles server software with NT. Little Web development freeware or shareware is available for NT, and what does exist will likely be buggy because the OS is so new that it's still tricky to write software for. In fact, due to Windows' youth, many of the programs for sale from Microsoft itself are likely to be buggy, and Microsoft technical support doesn't have a great reputation in the business world.

The PC hardware can cost from $2,000 to over $10,000, depending on speed of the processor, amount of random access memory, and hard drive size. Expect to pay about $1000 for the NT software, which includes server software.

CASE STUDY

Operational Technologies: Opting for Windows

The main reason that Carl Haywood chose Windows NT Work Station to serve Operational Technologies' Web site was to save money on hardware. The environmental engineering service company has three Novell servers, a Lotus Notes server, and three UNIX servers in addition to the NT workstation. "We were using our UNIX boxes for other things and didn't want to buy a new one," Haywood says. "The expense was twice the cost of a comparable PC. Plus this is easier and quicker to set up."

Haywood bought a Pentium 90 with 32 megabytes of RAM and one gigabyte of hard-drive disk space. The only thing the computer runs is NT Workstation, which Haywood bought because it was cheaper than NT Server software; it also takes less RAM and disk space to run. He paid $2,500 for the computer, $275 for the Microsoft NT Workstation software, and about $500 for O'Reilly & Associates' WebSite Server software.

"We did have some problems. We tried to install NT on an AST Bravo Computer, but there was an IBM chip in it, and Microsoft wouldn't install on an IBM chip even though the computer was on their list of approved computers," says Haywood, who had to spend some money on technical support. "I chafe at paying Microsoft $150 an incident for technical help. When you buy the product, you kind of feel like they should give you tech help on the first installation for free."

Another problem was the twenty disks that the Microsoft software came on, Haywood says. "I'd suggest the CD-ROM version." He also suggests buying more computer than you need up front. "It's like buying a house—buy as much as you can right now because you'll always run out later." Graphics in particular eat up disk space, as do programs that run customer support functions like providing technical help answers for customers to download. To maximize the available disk space, Haywood runs only the Web site on this computer. "We don't want a employee sitting there on the machine, saying, 'Oops, I deleted this. Oops, I turned the power off.' "

The company has maximized the computer's storage space, but that doesn't help the fact that it's connected to a 28.8 baud modem—a speed more suitable for home computers than businesses. "We need a bigger pipe," Haywood says. "It's phenomenal that we're running the whole company off what people use at home." Email, file downloading, and Web site traffic are all funneled through the same small phone line. "You just can't get a whole bunch of people on there at once," he says. "When there's five or six of us using it, you notice. That's why our page doesn't have a whole lot of graphics on it. The 28.8 modem was one of our design constraints."

"I would buy the same thing today," Haywood says of his software and hardware choices. "In fact, we're going to upgrade to the new version of WebSite Server."

Macintosh

Macintosh's famous point-and-click interface is even easier to use than Windows NT, and the OS costs about the same. While UNIX is infamous for being easy to hack, the design of Macintosh makes it almost impossible to get into parts of the computer the owner wants to protect. By 1996, no one had yet hacked a Macintosh. It's probably not necessary to hire a computer expert to program and administer the Web site on Macintosh—AppleScript programming language is English-based and user-friendly.

On the down side, not many businesses use Macintosh computers, so there's less business software available for it than for Windows or UNIX. Because of that, Web programmers are predicting that UNIX and Windows NT will be the hot systems for Web development in the future.

A PowerPC or Quadra with 32 to 40 megabytes of RAM and a two-gigabyte hard drive will cost about $2,000 to $2,500; WebSTAR server software is about $500.

CASE STUDY

Sweetwater Sound: Serving on Macintosh

When Chuck Surack began researching the Web in early 1995, there weren't many options for using Macintosh computers to serve in-house Web sites. But the CEO of Sweetwater Sound, a high-end music and recording equipment retailer, had been using Macs exclusively since 1984. "We had such an investment in Macs that the deciding factor for us was the familiarity we have with the interface," he says. "We knew we could be more productive quicker with a Mac, without having to invest time in learning a new system and interface."

At that time, computers from Silicon Graphics International (SGI) were the hot computers for Web serving. "There was a buzz about it, so for about two seconds we considered using a Silicon Graphics machine," he says. "They had all the tools to develop pages. It was a turnkey solution." The SGI computer would have run server software for UNIX but not for Macintosh. "The hard part for Mac was that there weren't software tools readily available. It was difficult to find server and design software," Surack says. "But the more we looked into it, we found shareware and stuff that was about to be released." The PowerMac 6100 was about half the price of the SGI package that Surack was considering, and it was easier to network with Sweetwater's existing one hundred Macintoshes. That, plus the huge labor savings in already knowing the system, convinced Surack to stick with Macintosh.

He spent about $7,000 for the PowerMac 6100, WebSTAR software from StarNine (a division of Quarterdeck), and several Web authoring software packages. Sweetwater already owned a scanner and digital camera. "We bought different software packages and put the pieces together ourselves," says Surack. After debuting the site in May 1995, Surack upgraded the server to an Apple 6150, Macintosh's workgroup server. In the fall of 1995, he bought an even faster machine, a PowerMac 8100/80 with 40 megabytes of RAM. Setting up the PowerMac and configuring it for designing and maintaining the Web site took only a few hours. "We spent three months learning about the Web and making sure being on it made sense," Surack says. "It's obvious today, but a year ago you wondered if it would take off. When we decided to do it, sixty days later we had the Web site."

The biggest challenge to serving the site on a Macintosh platform has been finding service providers to hook up and maintain the modem lines. "Most of the network providers are used to big expensive computers and firewalls," Surack says. "It was difficult finding a provider who could make things work at the other end with the Mac."

"It's been an incredibly good investment for us," Surack says. "We get four hundred new customers a month from it, and the salary and expenses to maintain it aren't more than $4,000 per month. When I buy a page ad in an industry magazine, I pay more than that, and only get fifty to one hundred leads."

Designing a Site

The basic tool for Web design is HyperText Markup Language, (HTML) used to code the Web page elements. For example, say a site should read, "The lowest prices in Cyberspace," with "lowest" in boldface type. Using HTML, a designer would type in "The <b>lowest</b> prices in Cyberspace." The <b> and </b> codes tell the browser that looks at the site to turn the boldface type on, then off, respectively. It's a fairly easy programming language to use, so most professional Web designers still rely on it. The HTML editing software is free to anyone who wants to download it from the Internet, or developers can simply learn the code and create a text file to store it.

Web design software is available to make HTML prettier and easier to use for nonprogrammers; the raw text the designer is coding looks more like the finished Web site. Some, called "export utilities," work with word processors like Microsoft Word or Novell's WordPerfect. Designers create the site in the word processor software, then send the site to the export utility to be translated into HTML. The disadvantage to using these is that some HTML features (like text wrapped around a graphic, or bulleted lists) don't always translate completely, so the page won't look the way it was originally designed. Some extra time and finessing may be necessary to achieve the desired effect.

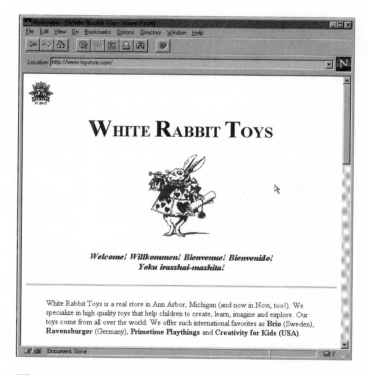

White Rabbit Toys designed an attractive site easily, using inexpensive Web design software.

Another type of design software are WYSIWYG (what you see is what you get) editors. With this type of software, designers use pull-down menus to design the site (i.e., for creating bold text, there's a "bold" option from the menu across the top of the screen). The software is very easy to use, but one problem is that it won't create a page to match exactly what you'll see on the Web. To see the finished site, designers must actually look at it with a Web browser.

For companies determined to build and serve a Web site in-house, design expertise is the one thing to consider handing over to someone else. As more and more sites open on the Web, the struggle to be noticed heats up. A professionally designed site can give a company an edge over a competitor with a poorly planned site. After all, most visitors try a site only once. If they don't like it, they never go back. By outsourcing only the initial design, a company still retains control of the process, since it's a short-term job subject to company approval, and once the site is up and running, the company has complete

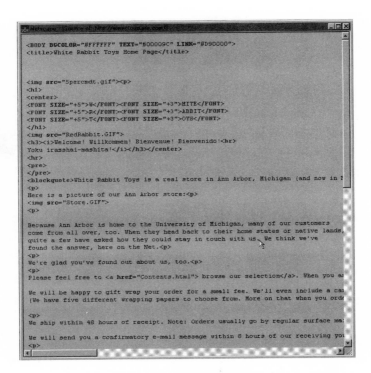

The source code that White Rabbit Toys used to design the Web site. These codes are so simple to use that most Web site designers still work with them rather than fancier software packages.

control over updates and changes. In fact, to save money, a company can outsource the design and pay a designer for printed mock-up pages of the site. The company can then implement the design themselves in-house.

After choosing a software operating system and Web development software, the next step is site design. The fastest and cheapest way to develop a design is for one person in the company to handle it. That person should choose several existing sites that they like and pinpoint what's attractive about them: Are they easy to navigate? Quick to download? Colorful and attention-getting? Useful sources of information? Make a list of the important elements the company wants to include in its site. Then copy the software programming codes used to design the site ("source codes" can be copied easily with a command in the Web browser software). Once the source code is copied, it's easy to copy other useful parts of many sites to create a site that utilizes the best features of them all. Many designers work this way, even professional ones. Just don't copy any one site too faithfully or you may be violating copyright law, as one designer found out.

CASE STUDY

White Rabbit Toys: Stopping a Copycat Site

In the fall of 1994, Bob Lilienfeld created a Web site for White Rabbit Toys, his wife JoAnne's small retail shop in Ann Arbor, Michigan. A year later he was checking out his competitors' Web sites, searching Yahoo's listings for the keywords "toy stores." While Lilienfeld chatted on the phone, he clicked on one address to link to a site. "I saw the site and said, 'Hey, I don't remember punching my own URL,' " he says. "I looked more closely and realized this other site had downloaded our source code and just put in their name."

Lilienfeld fired off an email message to the other site, saying, "Lovely site. Unfortunately, it looks exactly like ours." When he checked back a few days later, he says, "They had changed one page but nothing else." A friend who was a copyright attorney advised Bob and JoAnne that they had grounds for a lawsuit. He offered to write a letter to the copycat site and see what happened.

"I thought there would be a fight," Lilienfeld says. "But we got a letter back saying they were sorry, and they'd stop. They wanted to sign an agreement." A settlement was reached within a matter of weeks, and the offending site changed their design and paid White Rabbit's legal fees. "The fact that they changed the site so quickly and asked for a settlement document means they knew they had made a mistake," he says. "I know they had a designer, and I suspect he saw our site and thought it would make his job a lot easier to copy it. I doubt the store owner knew that his site had been copied word for word from ours.

"I was glad I found out about it before the Christmas rush, when the most damage could have occurred," Lilienfeld says. "Winning a settlement strengthens our rights to what we've done and sets a small legal precedent regarding copyright on the Web."

Copying another site isn't the only legal issue. Another is using copyrighted material. Any previously published or printed material—graphics, text, or design elements—could already be copyrighted. A company that wants to use such material must secure the rights from whoever created it. When in doubt, ask. Legal experts say that copyright infringement cases are very easy to prove and difficult to defend.

Design Issues and Tools

The most important thing to remember about design is that most visitors are reaching the site using modems, not leased lines. Those modems are slow, and the people using them are impatient. They don't like to wait for anything to download. Even if it's the most exciting interactive graphic on the entire Web, if it takes too long to download, nobody will bother to do it a second time. The classic mistake many small companies make is to include a large company logo or scanned photographs of employees on the first page of their Web site. Color graphics take up the most storage space on the computer, and also take much longer to download than text. By the time customers complain to the company about the download time, it's too late to recapture those visitors who left without complaining. Before debuting any Web site, make sure to view it using a slow modem connection—14.4 baud or less. (More on designing to attract visitors in chapter 7.)

The second thing to be aware of is that the design process takes time. Many CEOs who begin designing and maintaining their company's Web sites soon find it takes most of their to time to keep it current and interesting. At some point, every company needs to appoint or hire a "Webmaster" to take over; some simply hire that person at the start to create the site.

Companies that want to outsource all or part of building and serving their Web sites don't have to worry as much about hardware, software, phone lines, and design details. They do have to worry about finding reliable consultants and Web site developers. They also have to decide if they'll outsource the whole project or just part of it, and if they'll one day bring the site in-house if it's successful. These issues are discussed in chapter 5.

5

● ●

Recruiting Experts:
Outsourcing Your Site

Companies can choose from two approaches when building and maintaining a Web site. Keeping the whole process in-house offers the most control, but it is also the most expensive (see chapter 4). Outsourcing part or all of a site to professionals is less expensive and is the most common approach that small companies take. Many choose to outsource the maintenance, or serving, of the site but design and maintain it in-house. ("Hybrid" sites like these are discussed later in the chapter.) Outsourcing is popular for several reasons, the most appealing of which is the lower cost compared to doing it in-house. For the average small company with a modest amount of technical expertise on staff, it's pretty expensive to invest in hiring technical labor just to create a Web site. Hiring consultants to handle it saves money on what, for many companies, is a marketing expense. Companies that outsource point out that they wouldn't try to print their brochures and catalogs in-house, so why try to serve a Web site?

Outsourcing leaves the company free focus on its core competency instead of veering off into the online industry. If experts are monitoring the Web site, the company's employee workload is decreased. Creating and maintaining a good Web site requires plenty of online surfing to see what else is going on out there, but it's sometimes difficult to tell if employees are browsing sites that are useful to the company or just those that are fun to play with. Paying a professional who's already up to speed on Web developments saves time on the learning curve because the professional already knows more about the Web than your employees do. Paying a service company to store the site saves money on hardware upgrades—the server company, not you, worries about having enough computer power to handle your site.

Another increasingly compelling reason is the heightened competition for attention on the Web. The more sites that go online, the more pressure there is to have a well-done, attractive site. Consumers increasingly expect sophisticated design and transaction capability from a site. With the development of special effects from Java and VRML, it's becoming more important to jazz up a site, and more difficult to develop such a site without professional assistance. And even though the site is stored somewhere outside the company, you can still have your own personalized URL—visitors can reach your site at www.mycompany.com.

Outsourcing's biggest disadvantage is loss of control over the site. You have to wait for someone else to make changes and updates. You may not even own the rights to certain parts of the site. For some companies, this is a major concern—enough to make the in-house serving and development investment. If control is the most important issue at your company, bring the Web site in-house. If money is the main issue, consider outsourcing.

Who Should Outsource?

If you're still not sure which solution is best for your company, read through this checklist. If you can identify with two or more of these statements, read on. Outsourcing is probably your smartest move.

We don't have a lot of computer experts on staff: Either your company would have to hire someone to create the Web site, or in-house staffers would have to spend quite a bit of time getting up to speed learning about the Web. That's a sizable investment in labor. To do a rough comparison, first calculate what outsourcing would cost: Call a few Web developers and ask about their rates—some charge hourly, some charge flat fees based on the project. Although a developer's hourly rate is probably more than an in-house employee's, assume that the developer will take half as long to create the site as an untrained in-house person or new hire. Add to that expense a certain amount of staff labor cost for frequent meetings with the consultant during the few months it will take to create the Web site. Then add the cost to hire at least a part-time employee after the site opens to tackle the tasks the ISP can't handle, like answering company email and searching out compatible links for the site.

Compare that total cost to the expense of developing and storing the site in-house. Development time will take at least twice as long; then add the cost of a full-time employee to process email and find links, plus the administrative tasks the ISP would normally handle, such as buying hardware and software, dealing with the phone company, forwarding email, processing orders, and ensuring the site is always up and running. Add the cost of the hardware, software, and phone lines. (For a sample estimate, see the cost comparison chart later in this chapter.)

Once the site opens, someone will always have to be on call in case the computer that houses the site shuts down and your visitors can't reach it. Or in case the phone lines go down. Or in case someone hacks the system and breaks into the network. The risk of hacking is still fairly rare, and sites and phone lines don't shut down all that frequently, but a contingency plan (just as the companies that handle outsourced sites have) is essential in case it happens. At most small companies serving sites in-house, it's the CEO who handles this responsibility. For a CEO or a sales/marketing director who does all of a company's new market development, this investment of time might make sense. If not, then outsource.

We're not yet sure if a Web site is worth it. We want to see some results first: At six months? A year? Fix a decision point. Set goals for the site, and at your chosen decision point, evaluate whether or not it's reaching those goals. If so, it's probably time to bring the site in-house for more control and experimentation. If not, rethink the site. Either it's the wrong kind of site for the desired goals, or it's too early in your industry to have one. Because serving in-house is more expensive than outsourcing, both up-front and in monthly labor costs, be sure the site is working before investing in that move.

We don't have a leased phone line or any spare computers: Hardware, software, and phone lines are the smallest expense and shouldn't be the determining factor in the decision. In fact, companies that don't have the equipment to maintain the site aren't prohibited from designing it. Many small companies design the site on an in-house computer, then outsource the storage to their ISP's computers. More on this "hybrid" type of site at the end of the chapter.

We need a Web site up and running really quickly: Perhaps your competitors are already online and making you nervous. Maybe a large customer has asked for Web interaction capability, or you're speaking at an industry trade show and want to be able to mention your online strategy. Whatever the reason, a Web designer can get a basic site up and running more quickly than you can, because that's his or her core business. Once it's up, you can work on fine-tuning it if it's not perfect. But if you decide you have to have a site up this month, outsourcing is the way to go.

We won't be making a whole lot of changes to the site once it's up: Catalog sites, or any that offer products or services for sale, require frequent updates on listings and prices. If yours is more of a "here is who we are" promotional type site, your company will be making fewer monthly changes. Each of those change costs extra for sites that outsource but not for in-house sites with a Webmaster on staff. So the fewer changes your company will be making, the more reason to outsource.

We have no database or corporate documents we want to link to the site: If your company wants to link a database of products to the site so that all Web site product searches and purchases are made from a current product list, you'd have to store the Web site in-house. The database and the Web site have to be stored on the same computer for maximum efficiency, and putting both on an ISP's computer requires too much maintenance to keep the database current. If your company has a fairly straightforward site that doesn't have to be linked to the company in any way, outsource it.

If, after analyzing labor and maintenance requirements, your company decides that outsourcing is more cost-effective, don't rule out eventually bringing the site in-house. Companies that think they might do this one day should bear this in mind when signing contracts with the designer and server company. Otherwise, someone else might end up owning part of your company's site, and you can't take it with you when you move. It's also important to spell out in the contract that the ISP or developer will cooperate with the move, providing necessary technical expertise for the transition. More on this later in this chapter.

Cost Analysis: Outsourcing Versus In-House Serving

Before making the decision, it's useful to compare expenses. This cost analysis is a general outline based on sixty-five small companies who supplied their cost information for this book. For the companies interviewed—ranging from manufacturing to retail, and covering both high and low-tech industries—the average site took 2.6 months to create from inception to debut on the Web. Use these cost categories as guidelines for running your own cost analysis.

DEVELOPMENT EXPENSES

OUTSOURCED SITE		IN-HOUSE SITE	
Designer	$13,000	Employee building the site	$15,000
ISP sign-up fee	$100	Hardware (modems and computers)	$9,000
		Software	$4,000
		Phone line installation	$1,000
Total:	$14,000	Total:	$29,000

MONTHLY MAINTENANCE EXPENSES

OUTSOURCED SITE		IN-HOUSE SITE	
Site storage fees	$900	Leased phone line service	$1,200
Designer/ISP to make		Employee labor to maintain	
ongoing changes	$300	the site	$5,000
Employee labor to answer			
email and find suitable			
links for site	$3,000		
Total:	$4,200	Total:	$6,200

Bear in mind that not every Web site is created equal—some will take more time and cost more money to create than others. For example, the labor costs of developing a Web site (either in-house or outsourcing) will be higher than these estimates if the company runs testing periods before opening the site and makes frequent changes during the site's development phase. And very few Web sites debut without having undergone at least a few incarnations along the way. Another factor affecting price is a company's geographic area. This particularly affects phone costs, which sometimes vary widely across parts of the country. Web site storage fees will vary according to the ISP's location and the level of service offered; monthly fees in this survey ranged from $30 to several thousand dollars. Another issue to think about is the experience and skill levels of the developers and company employees—it can make a big difference in the cost of setting up a site. Even an experienced designer will have to spend quite a bit of time educating managers who haven't seen the Web before, but that designer can jump right into concept discussions if people at the company have invested a little time browsing the Web beforehand.

Finding Service Providers

It's a good idea to find a service provider before shopping for a developer. Many ISPs also offer Web development service, for one-stop shopping. Those that don't can frequently recommend reliable designers. A good way to start the search is by calling the ISPs in your company's area and asking if they serve business Web sites—ones that do are often called "Web farms" or "server farms." Asking other company owners or computer specialists for the name of the ISP that serves their Web site will turn up even better prospects. Bear in mind that the ISP doesn't necessarily have to be in your company's geographic area to serve the site. Large ISPs like UUNET and PSINet serve Web sites for companies all over the country. Once you've narrowed the field to a few ISPs that sound promising, set up interviews with the customer service representative, or the owner if it's a small company. These are the key questions to ask and the options to consider:

What type of service do you offer?   Web farms are companies that run rooms full of computers where they store their customers' Web sites. There are several different ways the sites are stored. The most common is one site per computer, which means that your company's site is stored on its own computer. Nothing else is on that computer except perhaps some firewall software (which offers protection against hackers); some Web farms will run firewall software for the whole farm on one separate computer. At some Web farms, the company's site is stored on one computer and the graphics for that site on another, which makes the site download faster for visitors.

The second—and cheaper—option is to share a computer with other sites. Your company's site can still have its own domain name, like "www.mycompany. com," so visitors can't tell that the site is on a shared computer miles away from your offices. The site is separated from the other domains on the same computer by server software. The disadvantage to this is if one of those other sites gets a lot of traffic, your site will slow down and be more difficult to access. Also, if someone decides to hack one of those other sites, your site is also at risk.

The newest option is to lease an empty computer—referred to as "co-location." A Web farm houses several computers that share T1 phone lines. The computers are basically empty boxes, with no server software on them. The company not only stores their Web site on the computer but also their own server software. Someone in the company serves the site remotely, calling the Web farm computer up with a modem line and thereby tracking visitors, making changes, and fixing bugs. In this case, the service the Web farm provides is merely monitoring the hardware and phone lines and fixing them if something goes wrong. Because they don't provide any other services, this option is fairly inexpensive and attractive for hybrid sites.

How big is your pipe to the Internet?   The size (or speed) of the ISP's phone line connection to the Internet is part of what determines how quickly Web users will be able to download the sites at that ISP. Some large ISP companies, like BBN or UUNET, run the computers that make up the central Internet backbone. Companies like this have the fastest connections available, because there are no phone lines to connect them to the Internet—they're actually part of the Internet. The next best thing is a T3 line connecting the ISP to the Internet. (A T1 is the next largest, and then a 56K line.) Some companies offer shared, or fractional, phone lines, in which more than one company is using the T1 or T3 line. It's cheaper than the full line but can also be slower. (More on phone line speeds and configuration options in chapter 3.)

What's your disaster plan?   When a Web site is down, visitors get an error message that tells them simply that their browser can't find the site. The Web user doesn't know if that's because the site doesn't exist, has moved, or is just experiencing temporary technical difficulty. That's why any company maintaining a Web site should have as its first priority keeping the site open and available to visitors.

Most larger Web farms with corporate customers ensure this by having duplicate locations. For example, PSINet, a Web server company based in Herndon, Virginia, also has offices in California. Both locations have computers that mirror each other. All of the company Web sites stored in Herndon are backed up on the computers in California. If one or the other location were hacked, or a local disaster shut down the phone lines, PSINet's Web sites would still run from the alternate location. Any server company should at least have trained staff on call twenty-four hours a day in case there are any problems in the computer room, and your company should be given the name of someone at the ISP to call at any time. The ISP should charge less per month if they expect you to handle any problems with the phone company. If they handle hooking up and maintaining the phone lines, expect to pay a bit more. If the ISP doesn't offer these services, they're probably more of a consumer-focused company, not used to serving business sites.

Have your sites ever been hacked?   Don't rule out a company that answers "yes." In fact, a company with computers that have been broken into, and that then took steps to prevent it from happening again, is probably safer than one that's never been hacked and isn't sure of its protection. If a company has good firewall protection that's been tested—whether by a certified hacker or by someone paid to try hacking it—then it's as safe as anything else on the Internet.

Do you handle transactions and visitor tracking?   Even if your company isn't planning to process transactions right away, it probably will in the future. "Transaction" doesn't just mean sales. Your company might want to offer an interactive form on which visitors type some kind of information, then send it to you. You'll want to assure them that this information is confidential and secure. "Tracking" reports are the records of visitors who visit the site and when. Some ISPs only offer "hit rates," which aren't very reliable numbers (more on this in chapter 8). Others offer tracking reports that tell, among other things, how many visitors go to the site, where they're from (schools, government organizations, commercial accounts, online services), how long they stay, what parts of the site they look at and for how long, and if they've been to the site before. Ask the server company for a sample report, and ask them to spell out what information is available.

What upgrades and changes will you handle?   Most server companies will make a few changes to the site each month without charging customers additional fees, but they should spell out what those changes are and how quickly they'll make them. Will they scan a graphic image into the computer to add to the site, for example? Will they adjust the site's inventory listings if your company runs out of or adds a particular product? Many won't. What they won't do, you'll have to do in-house or hire a designer for, and both will cost additional money.

What's the size limit for my site?   It's difficult to judge how large or small a site is just by looking at it. Graphics and colors take up more computer space than text. So a three-page site with lots of colorful graphics can be a larger computer file than a ten-page site with mostly text. In general, you don't want your site to be limited to any fewer than two megabytes. A thirty-page color site with small graphics on each page should fit easily into two megabytes. Most likely you'll want to add more to the site as it's used, so allow room to grow by securing more space now than your site needs.

How much will this cost? Some servers charge by the "hit," or visitor. Some charge by the size of the site, and some charge by the month. Monthly fees range from $15 to $1,000, depending on the phone line speed and level of service your company expects. Toward the lower end of the range, ISPs don't provide any extra services like tracking reports, transaction processing, or warnings when the server will be down. At the upper end of the range, expect a fat phone line and every service possible—this should be a Web farm specializing in catering to business sites.

Do you have a standard contract? What terms does it address? Every company should have a contract with their server that spells out what parts of the site the company can take if it leaves. Some server companies that handle the transaction processing for their clients retain the rights to the transaction section of the site, so companies that take the site elsewhere must find a new way to process sales. If you think your company might eventually move the site, ask if the server company might help select hardware and software—and include those terms in the contract. You also should ensure in the contract that all of your site's data, including tracking reports, is confidential. If the contract doesn't spell out that these reports should be seen only by your company, an eager ISP might use them to impress a prospective client—maybe one of your competitors.

Another issue to spell out in the contract is response time. Be clear about your expectations for how quickly someone at your company will be notified if there's a problem with the site, how soon a technician will begin working on it, and how long before you can expect either a solution or a price discount on your service.

It's important to negotiate contracts with designers as well. Some keep the rights to graphics they create for the site, though they may release those rights for a higher fee. You should make clear in the contract that the designer is responsible for securing all rights to any material used in the site. Otherwise, your company could be held responsible if the designer scans in copyrighted material from a publication or another site.

What platform are you serving on? It doesn't matter much while your company's site is with the server company, but if you move the site (whether in-house or to another server company), it does. The site can easily be moved to another computer with the same operating system—whether that's Windows NT, UNIX, Macintosh, or some other software. Most industry analysts feel that Windows and UNIX are the server platforms of the future, so choosing a server company using one of those means that most likely there won't be any trouble moving the site later.

CASE STUDY

PhotoDisc: Negotiating Contracts

Tom Hughes designed his company's first Web site in late 1994 but outsourced the maintenance. The ISP had contracts with only a few clients; PhotoDisc was one of them. Hughes says that early contract focused mostly on performance issues: "They had to notify us of problems within an hour, and if the site was down more than three times for total time greater than an hour over a span of a few days, we got a fee reduction." Hughes's monthly fee was based on the volume his site took up on the ISP's computer.

That site is a lot larger now and served by a different ISP. PhotoDisc sells photographs directly from the Web site, which it didn't do on the first site. Now clients can order what photos they like and download them immediately. "If this site is down, we could really lose business," Hughes says. So he insisted on better terms in his second contract. The ISP has to notify Hughes within thirty minutes if the site is down, and they must get support staff working on the problem just as quickly.

What has he learned about negotiating Web contracts? "Negotiating the cost is critical if you need a lot of storage space," he says. "Also, really focus on the system the ISP has in place for performance and data tracking, and make sure they can deliver it in a form that can go directly into your accounting system or database." It can be expensive to adjust an in-house software system to fit an ISP's reporting system. Also, says Hughes, don't be afraid to negotiate, even with an ISP or designer that has a standard contract.

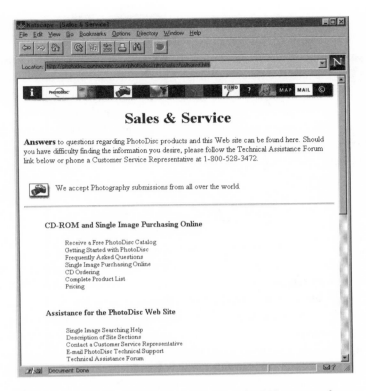

PhotoDisc couldn't afford to lose any sales if the Web site was down. The company negotiated a contract with their service provider that addressed that concern.

Finding Designers

Your company has decided to outsource the site, but how to find the right people? Lately it seems like everyone is doing Web development work, many with no prior experience. The best way is to cruise the Web and see who designs and maintains sites that are easy to navigate or are in the same industry as your company. Most Web sites have the name of the designer somewhere on the site. Frequently it's also a hypertext link that takes visitors who click on it to that designer's home page. From there it's easy to send email or write down the designer's name and phone number and make a quick phone call. Another way to find designers is to ask your company's ISP for referrals. Most ISPs, if they don't have designers on staff, have a few to whom they refer work.

After locating a few designers, here are some questions that can help narrow the field:

Can you meet our deadline?   The best design team in the world is of no use if they can't meet a deadline. If your company's site must be up and running by a fixed deadline (in time for a trade show or a budget period, for example), that should be the first question to the designers. If they say they can meet it, make sure that issue is addressed in the contract. Each day the project is late should be reflected by a discount in the price. It's not unreasonable to expect a design team to have a working site ready to go within a month—if they have good communication with the company they're designing for and with the ISP, if there aren't many levels of approval for the site to pass through, and if there's no need for a test period. Set up mini-deadlines along the way, to make sure everyone understands how the site should progress.

Can I see some samples of your work?   Ask for samples even from designers who's work you've already seen on the Web. A savvy design team will show samples of work they've done for companies in your industry, or companies that are similar to your company's size, or that sell similar products. Look for variety in the sites. Is the designer using different solutions for different sites, or is the designer just repeating one standard design trick? Don't look for examples of designs that would work for your company's site. Look instead for design solutions that work for the site they're on. Designers who are able to show another business site to its best advantage can likely do the same for yours.

Are you the people who will do the actual work?   Some busy design firms farm some projects out to another designer, sometimes a freelancer who's not even on staff. That's not necessarily a problem. Just be sure to meet the person or people who will actually be doing the grunt work on your company's site. You'll be in many meetings with them as the site develops, so make sure there's good communication before committing to them.

What other services do you provide?   If there's nobody in-house or at the company's ISP who can do upgrades and maintenance on the site, think about structuring an agreement with the designers. What will they charge to make regular updates, such as pricing changes, adding new products and removing old ones, or updating links to other sites? How often can they make these changes: Daily? Weekly? How much will it cost to add new pages or scan in additional graphics? All of these details should be spelled out in the contract. Other services they might provide include finding a service provider and registering a company domain name.

Can you work with our in-house technical people? If someone in-house at your company will help design the site, establish up front how involved that person will be with the designers. If that person can write in HTML, ask the designers if they're available to just organize the site, then pass the plan along to the in-house person for the actual creation. Will they later work to upgrade that design if necessary?

When can we see a mock-up? If there are several designers you like, consider paying them to create mock-ups of the site for comparison. Use those samples to decide which designer to choose. These mock-ups should look like little flow charts, showing how visitors would progress from one page to the next and where links to outside pages might be. Don't expect fancy graphics and meaningful text—the samples should mostly illustrate how users would navigate your Web site.

How much will this cost? Designers price themselves many different ways. Some charge by the project, some by the hour, and some by the page. Hourly rates range from $30 to $100, usually depending on the experience level of the designer but not necessarily. Because it's a new industry, there's no pricing standardization yet. The cheapest designers are those without much experience, willing to take on their first client at a discount rate in return for the finished product to list on their resume. Many small companies gamble on untried designers. It's risky—stories of missed deadlines and disappearing designers abound. But some get lucky. Hot Hot Hot's site was the first created by Presence, a start-up Palo Alto, California, design firm. Hot Hot Hot got a discount, Presence got a site to show to future clients, and the colorful, eye-catching site got a lot of attention from consumers and in the media.

CASE STUDY

Zaske, Sarafa and Associates: Finding a Deal on a Design Service

The designer that Haithem Sarafa hired to develop Zaske, Sarafa and Associates' Web site now charges twice what he charged the $6 million financial services company in late 1995. Sarafa found P. J. Stafford at the Internet Factory when he was

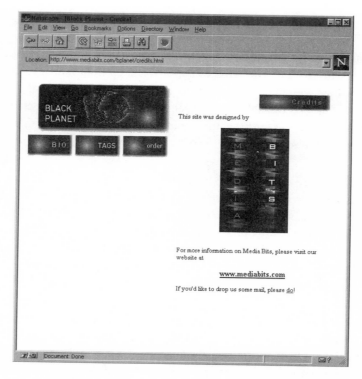

Look for the developer's name on well-designed Web sites. This is an easy way to find referrals.

looking for a client in their industry. Sarafa was able to work out an inexpensive deal for the site's design, storage, and maintenance. Price and location were the deciding factors— Stafford's was the lowest quote they received, and he was located only two blocks away from Sarafa's Birmingham, Michigan, office. They signed a contract, and Zaske, Sarafa and Associates got a six-page Web site in just over a month.

"We were his twentieth customer but his first financial-industry customer," Sarafa says. "He was looking for an entry into the financial services market." Sarafa asked for work samples, which showed that Stafford knew not only the Web but his clients' business. "He understood the clients enough to suggest what types of links may be important," says Sarafa. "And he had done a lot of marketing for clients, announcing the site."

Sarafa commissioned a preliminary proposal. Stafford developed a sample site with two full pages and an outline of which topics would be covered in several more pages. Sarafa paid $500 for the project up front, deciding only after it was delivered to commit to a full site. He set up checkpoints during the process in case the project might start to lag or veer off in the wrong direction. He ended up paying $2,800 for the six-page site, plus $15 per month for storage and minor text changes. "We had quotes in the $8,000 to $10,000 range," says Sarafa. Shopping around paid off for the company. "We're still with him. He checks with me every few months, sending a current page and asking if we'd like any updates."

The Absolute Cheapest Solution

Outsourcing is cheaper than building a site in-house, but building a site that's a hybrid of both is the cheapest of all. The company designs it in-house, then serves it with a local Internet access provider—the one that may already service the company's email account. Most ISPs offer limited Web site storage space, geared mostly toward consumers interested in putting up a personal home page. Companies that are willing to store their business site there can save money, because the Web space is included in the monthly email service charges. The company can also save time—by designing it in-house and making all the decisions without calling any meetings, a company can have a site up and running fairly quickly. Then it's easy to make changes at any time, without contacting a design firm or ISP to schedule it. A designated person at the company simply logs on to the Web site from a computer at the company, keys in a special password assigned by the ISP, and then makes the changes.

One drawback to a hybrid site is that the ISP probably isn't prepared to serve a business Web site. Therefore they aren't concerned about what happens to corporate Web sites when they close Internet service for computer or phone line upgrades. The ISP probably won't provide tracking services, update the site, or help a company create it. That's one reason their storage service will be cheaper than service from Web farms that do offer those options. Another risk for a hybrid site is that it can look amateurish. A site that's difficult to navigate or doesn't offer any real value for visitors won't draw any repeat visitors. If, after spending time surfing the Web, nobody at the company is confident enough to create a useful, interesting site, don't try the hybrid approach. But if someone on staff does have a handle on basic design concepts, then a hybrid site is probably worth a shot, especially if these statements apply to your company:

I already have an email account: It doesn't matter which ISP the account is with, or even if it's an employee's personal home account. Most likely, that ISP provides some Web site storage at no additional charge to its monthly rate. That's storage space that your company can definitely use.

That HTML stuff doesn't scare me: Good, because you'll be spending quite a bit of time designing in HTML or in a software package that translates it from word processing or plain text software. Whether using a software package or just plain old HTML for designing the site, the best way to save money is for an employee to design the whole site.

I don't want to sink much money into this until we see where it's going: A hybrid site is the best solution for bootstrappers—companies pinching pennies wherever they can. If your company has more time than money—and what money there is goes to essentials like buying inventory—then build a hybrid site. The Web is more open to a do-it-yourself approach than more traditional forms of marketing. A company that might not try to design and print its own catalog can create its own Web site, and the site will look just as good as many of the others out there.

CASE STUDY

Tennis Warehouse: Creating a Hybrid Site

Drew Munster started his direct mail business, Tennis Warehouse, in early 1995. He bootstrapped his Web site like he bootstrapped his $700,000 company, doing as much work as he could himself and saving money wherever he could. What Munster created was a hybrid site. He designed it in-house himself on his company's Macintosh computers but outsourced the serving to his inexpensive local ISP, also located in San Luis Obispo, California.

"We chose them because they're the only one in town and fairly cheap," he says. "They charge thirty dollars per month for our email accounts." One megabyte of Web site storage is included in the price, and Munster pays an extra $2.50 per megabyte per month, buying a total of five. His online catalog site is just over 4 megabytes. "We weren't absolutely thrilled with the service provider," he says. "It was okay for email, but when the Web site was down, I didn't think very much of that." The service was so cheap that Munster put off going elsewhere for about a year. In mid 1996, he changed service providers to a company that can handle online sales transactions.

It took Munster only about ten hours to create his simple site, which is actually larger and more colorful than his print catalog. The paper catalog was a two-page black-and-white mailer with only three photographs, and it listed only some of the company's tennis products. The thirty-page Web site lists all of the products, with up to fifty photographs on any given day. Munster updates it himself every few days. He figures he's saved a few thousand dollars by designing and maintaining it himself instead of hiring a designer or in-house Web person. "Paying someone to do frequent maintenance can add up quickly."

The constant maintenance is the most time-consuming part of maintaining a Web site in-house, Munster says. "Your Web page and other forms of advertising need to be saying the same thing. If there's differing information, customers will find it." When the company makes demands on Munster, the Web site is often the first thing to let slip. "I have the technical skills to maintain it, so we wouldn't gain that much by outsourcing the site," he says. "I try to update the page a couple of times a week. But lately I've been running behind on almost everything, so mostly I've just been updating the specials on the site."

Because he was comfortable working with computer programming languages, Munster designed his site using straight HTML, the script for designing Web sites. But he advises anyone who's hesitant to spend time learning a raw programming language to use a software package like PageMill from Adobe to make the design process easier. "The strength is that you don't have to know any HTML because it creates it all for you," he says. "But the drawback is since you don't create the code, you can't be quite as exotic with the design."

So far, the site accounts for about 35 percent of Tennis Warehouse's sales, all made via phone calls or fax. "It's real solid growth for us," Munster says. Someone with a larger advertising budget might be happier investing some of that income into farming out the site's maintenance, but Munster doesn't intend to outsource any time soon. "We're an aggressive discounter," he says, "and every penny counts."

Using the Online Services

Another inexpensive serving option is to use the online services to create a site. Customers who already subscribe to America Online, for example, can design and store a small 2 megabyte Web site using their software. There are a few limitations. AOL doesn't offer online transaction capability or interactive forms; they also don't provide any tracking reports. The site can't violate AOL's "terms of service," so a customer couldn't, for example, sell pornographic comic books. And sites created using AOL's software can't be moved to another server later—whether in-house or outsourced.

A site created and served by AOL or Prodigy is also available to visitors on the Web. Anyone with Web access can reach it, not just the online service subscribers, so in that respect it's just like having an independent Web site. If the

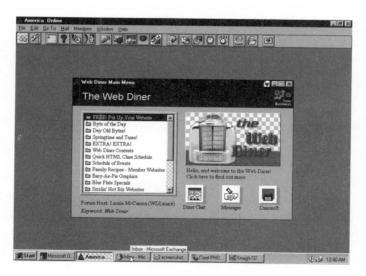

The online services offer easy-to-use Web site creation tools, with some limitations.

site lives up to your company's expectations—receiving a certain amount of email requests for company information, for example—then consider designing a similar site to store at another location that can be larger than 2 megabytes and accommodate online transactions.

Anyone developing a hybrid site should read chapter 4, on in-house serving and design. One thing your company will have to decide, whether designing a site in-house or outsourcing it to professionals, is what type of site you should have. There are several different models for Web sites. Many don't even offer products or services for sale, yet the companies are satisfied with the return on the Web investment. Next, we'll look at five models for Web sites, how they work, and a successful example of each one.

6

●●●●●●●●●●●●●●●●●●●●●●●●●●

What's My Line?:
Different Site Models

Any company can put up a successful, rewarding Web site. It doesn't matter whether it sells a product or service, whether that's sold to businesses or consumers, how long the sell cycle is, or how high or low the price. In fact, it doesn't matter whether the company sells at all—sales are secondary to the real attraction. The big secret that many companies haven't learned is that Web sites don't win visitors by offering things for sale, but by offering entertainment and information. The trick is simply to figure out what your company has that Web users are interested in. Sometimes that *is* a product; other times it's proprietary research data. Perhaps it's industry intelligence, customer service, cutting-edge Web site design, or entertaining writing that draws visitors to the site—only then will they buy something.

After pinpointing what will attract people to your company's Web site, the next step is to figure out how to feature it. There are many different models for successful business Web sites, and each one plays to the strength of the company using it. Catalogers offer online stores. Service companies create promotional sites. High-tech companies offer online customer service. Stuck for ideas for your company? Check out what others are doing; visit your competitors' sites. Once you have ideas from your industry, then look at the Web at large. Visit some popular sites to learn what's exciting and new in terms of design. The large search engine sites, like Yahoo! or Lycos, have "what's new" or "pick of the Web" lists to browse for current top sites.

To help decide what kind of site to build for your company, this chapter looks at five common models for business Web sites. Although there are other popular models—online shopping malls or job search sites, for example—many of those are being used by companies formed specifically as online businesses from the beginning. Rather than explore those, we're looking at the best options for existing companies. These models aren't mutually exclusive; some companies use combinations of several of them. We'll examine how these models work, whether or not they make money, and what kinds of companies can copy them. Then we'll profile a company that's using each model particularly well. Because every company is interested in making money online, let's first study an online store, or catalog.

The Online Store

It's as simple as its real-world store or catalog counterpart. Customers go to the store or pick up the catalog, browse the products, find an item they like, and purchase it. Most online stores offer products for sale. Some offer services, mostly those that can be performed or delivered electronically, like Aleph's online translation service (www.aleph.com). The biggest disadvantage to an online store as compared to a catalog is that it's still difficult to reach as many people online as through a print mailing list. Online, a company has to wait for customers to come to it instead of going to them with a mailer, so the ratio of orders to people who see the product list is usually lower than in print.

Fortunately, the production costs are also lower, so the return on investment can be much higher than with print. Online, there's no printer or postage to pay, and the cost of making changes to a Web site is much cheaper than ordering a print run of special sale inserts. Because a Web site can be changed at any moment, online inventory can be linked to the company's order-processing software so that real-time updates are performed automatically. When hats sell out, for example, they're instantly removed from the Web site. That's not possible with a print catalog.

But the most exciting thing product catalogers and stores can do online that's impossible for all but the smallest is to list their entire inventory. Imagine having room to show every product all the time in your catalog. When customers want to find something, they don't have to wander the aisles or flip through endless pages listing products by vague store department categories. Instead, they can type in keywords—"chocolate sauce" or "silver earrings"— and only those products appear on the page. That's what internal search engine software does, and it makes online shopping a breeze for customers.

Search engine software also opens doors for all sorts of one-to-one marketing possibilities. If a company wants to put advertisements on the site, those can be customized to each visitor. For example, say a visitor inputs the keywords "office chairs" in the search engine. When the list of chairs appears, the software can call up a pre-programmed ad for a certain type of chair on sale that week.

There are a few disadvantages to selling online. The classic catalog challenge is that customers can't interact with the merchandise online, so compelling copy and graphics have to do the selling. This same problem normally holds true for the Web, although music, video, artwork, software, and books can all be sampled online before purchase. Another online challenge is processing the actual transaction. Should your company take customer credit cards over the Internet? Pay instead for transaction services or software? Or just list a toll-free number for phone orders? (These options, and other ways of making money online, are discussed in more detail in chapter 9.)

The way an online store or catalog makes money is simple—profit from selling goods or services to customers. This doesn't mean that this type of site is limited to retailers. Business-to-business suppliers can have an online catalog. So can service companies that offer a service that can be performed or priced online.

CASE STUDY

Hot Hot Hot: Selling Online

In late 1994, Perry and Monica Bosserman Lopez opened a Web site for their three-hundred-square-foot hot sauce specialty shop and catalog in Pasadena, California, called Hot Hot Hot. By early 1996, the Web site was bringing in 20 percent of the store's $300,000 in retail and catalog sales.

The twenty-five page site is a burst of colorful computer graphics and hot sauce labels. All 450 products are online. "We

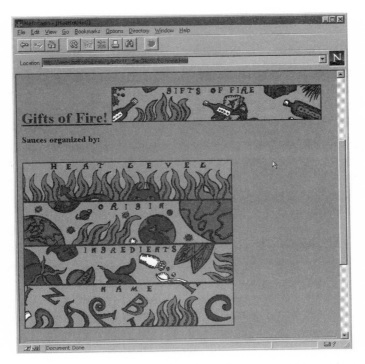

Hot Hot Hot's Web site is a mix of a catalog and online storefront, offering a searchable list of products for sale.

had to categorize them," Perry says, "otherwise it would be overwhelming. In a shop it's not so intense because there's more room." Visitors to Hot Hot Hot's Web site click on pictures of the sauces they're interested in and can read about where the sauce is from, its ingredients, and its heat level. "On the Web your selling tools are limited to text, graphics, and information flow," Monica says. "Ours is a food product, and customers can't touch or taste it. It becomes more an issue of providing information to create a need or desire for the product."

Customers who want to buy an item click on that option. A software program written by the company's Web developer, Presence, tracks the orders so that when the customer goes to the order page, all the chosen foods and sauces are listed automatically. The customer can then either print out the page and fax it to the store, call Hot Hot Hot's 800 number, or send the order form with a credit card number as email to Presence. Presence emails the customer to confirm the order, then prints out all orders daily and faxes them to Hot Hot Hot's warehouse. The small company couldn't afford encryption software (which secures online credit card orders) when the site debuted, so they decided to try sales without it. Although industry analysts warn that consumers are afraid to shop online, Perry and Monica haven't found that to be true. When the site first opened, about half of the online orders came over the telephone, half via unencrypted email. Now email orders are up to 75 percent. The shop receives and processes about ten orders a day from the Web site.

Usually one of those daily orders is from an overseas customer, which surprised Perry and Monica. "You're instantaneously a global company," Monica says. "Suddenly you have to figure out the best way to get things to Tel Aviv." Paying to ship products overseas is one of the disadvantages to selling online. Hot Hot Hot's first international order was to Great Britain, and the shipping costs blew the sale's profits. "We figured out a deal fast for the next day," says Monica. The store charges overseas customers the shipping fee plus a few dollars, and bills after the product is shipped.

When Perry first started exploring the idea of a Web site, he knew that their tiny retail shop couldn't afford to set one up in-house. When startup Web development company Presence approached him, he struck a deal. Presence, also located in Pasadena, charged $20,000 to create the site, with Hot Hot Hot paying that off as a percentage of online sales. Then the retailer continues to pay Presence 5 percent of online sales in return for about an hour each month of ongoing site maintenance, including design changes to the site. The fee also includes collecting and faxing email orders to the retailer's warehouse.

Selling online is more profitable than selling via catalog, with its high printing and mailing costs. Processing email orders is cheaper than paying for a toll-free phone order line. But getting customers to find the site and then return to it is tough. And the fact that the customer is the one who initiates and drives the sale is a big challenge, which Hot Hot Hot handles by trying to provide a captivating site with lots of product information and by interacting with visitors as much as possible. "The store is a totally personal experience—a customer can see, touch, smell, and taste what they are going to purchase. The salesperson is much more an active character," Monica explains. "There can be a real detached quality to ordering by computer, so it's important to respond to customer email. These customers want to know that you are really there."

The Lopezes hope to grow their online store, Monica says. "I would like it to be 50 percent of sales. We've talked about opening more retail sites, but that stretches us thinner," she explains. "Maybe we'll do another Web site instead, since we already have the mechanism down." Monica says that one online sale usually leads to another. "On the gift card orders, they write, 'Can you believe we ordered this from the Internet?' which is great word of mouth."

The Electronic Press Release

Putting up a list of consumer products and devising a way to process online sales is the most obvious kind of Web site. It's the kind that gets the most attention in the business world, because the expectation is that it will draw immediate—and often incremental—income. It has an easily measurable return. But not every company can, or should, put up this kind of site. For some, such as most service companies, transactions can't easily be made online. For other companies, like those heavily involved in research and development phases, there isn't even anything to sell. Some business models that exist in the real world, like a nightclub, don't seem to have any possible online counterpart. And yet, Alberto's Nightclub in Mountain View, California, has had a highly acclaimed and successful Web site since early 1994.

Alberto's Nightclub is a good example of a promotional site. Because people browsing the Web expect something new and different each day, this type of constantly changing Web site is ideal as a company promotional vehicle. Here's how a promotional site works: The company's site offers several areas of information that visitors can click on, like "who we are," "upcoming events," "job openings," and "click here to enter our vacation giveaway contest."

Company events, like new partnerships or a new market focus, can be announced on the Web site as soon as they happen, without the expense of sending out press releases. Contests and giveaway results can be updated continually. Job openings can be listed, pre-applications processed, and the ad removed as soon as the position is filled. Media contacts looking for basic company information can be referred to the Web site. And customer information, such as names and mailing addresses of those who visit the site, can be gathered quickly and easily.

The disadvantage to this type of site is that it doesn't replace traditional marketing. For a promotional site to work well, it's important to make sure that customers and prospects know about it. That still means relying on traditional marketing methods to point people to the Web site. List the URL on business cards, in print media advertisements, on letterhead, and in all print press releases. If customers regularly come in to your offices, promote the site there also. (For more tips on cheap promotion techniques, see chapter 7.)

Promotional sites don't offer goods or services for sale at the site, so they don't process transactions. Although the site doesn't make money through sales, it can often save the company money. For less than the cost of one magazine ad, a company can run a promotional Web site for a year. Posting media press releases on the Web site saves on mailing expense. Holding a one-time promotional event on the Web (such as offering a prize in return for customer registrations to build a mailing list) saves on mailing and the labor expense of hand-entering the registration information into a computer.

This kind of site can work well for consultants, professional services such as health care providers, accountants or lawyers, and nonprofits. It's also a good first site for companies just going online, who might then move to another model after an initial testing period of learning about the Web.

CASE STUDY

Alberto's Nightclub: Marketing and Promoting

Alberto's Nightclub has a Web site that is a glimpse of the future of online marketing. The $1 million dance club is in the heart of Silicon Valley, where most area employees work for high-tech companies and browse the Web all day. When owner Alberto Martin runs an ad or promotion for his club on the Web site, thousands of people see it, and hundreds of those go to the club. Today, a response like this is still limited to the few geographic areas that have high percentages of consumers using the Web regularly. But tomorrow, those geographic areas will be the

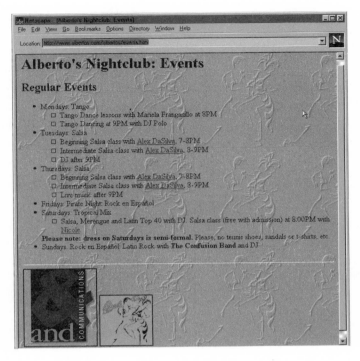

*Alberto's Nightclub lists monthly events and special promotions at the
Web site to publicize the club and attract visitors.*

rule, not the exception. And running an ad on the Web will be as
common for companies as buying space in the local newspaper.

Martin opened his Web site in early 1994. It's stored at his
local ISP for a bargain $600 per year. When Martin struck a
deal with the ISP, he was their first customer, so he was able to
negotiate a low price at a time when the Web was still in its
infancy. The ISP doesn't maintain or make changes to the site,
Martin does that himself once a week, sometimes outsourcing it
to a developer.

The site itself is about one hundred pages, including direc-
tions to the nightclub, pictures of the room, and fun features like
online salsa lessons. The main element is the simple event calendar. Every month, a new calendar goes up, listing all upcoming musical artists and special parties. Martin makes attending
these events more compelling for Web visitors with his online

special promotions. For example, frequently the nightclub offers discounted cover charges to patrons who email their reservations by a certain date. The customer gets a return email to print out and take to the nightclub as proof that the lower entry fee applies. Martin also started offering special email-only parties over a year ago. "We didn't know what kind of response we'd get," he says. "I figured a few people would come." So he waived the cover charge the first few times. The second time he offered it, he got two hundred responses from people coming to the three-hundred-person capacity club. Then, patrons only had to show up with a printout of the Web page invitation to get in. Now the twice-monthly nights are so popular that there's a cover charge, but it's lower for patrons with the printout.

"We got rid of our print mailing list," Martin says. Instead, he uses his three thousand-name electronic mailing list to keep patrons updated on upcoming events. This saves $1,500 per month in printing and mailing expenses, he says. "All it takes is my time to make up the messages and send them." Recently, Martin has started marketing to specific groups on his list. When he sees a lot of email addresses from a particular company, like "intel.com," he contacts the company (in this case, Intel) about holding a special party at the nightclub. So far, he's done several successful company nights.

"It's hard to tell who looks at your print ad," Martin says. But tracking reports from a Web site can effectively trace how many people look at the site and for how long. Martin promotes the Web site on all of his traditional marketing material, "The URL goes on our business cards, everything paper that we have." He also publicizes his event calendar elsewhere on the Internet, in the online discussion groups known as Usenet, where marketing can be tricky because commercialism is strongly frowned upon. "We post monthly on Usenet, but only to groups that might be interested. Mainly ones that deal with dance and music," Martin says.

Being able to leverage his electronic mailing list means that Martin saves on traditional marketing expenses. "We used to do more radio promotions," he says. "That can cost you $200 for thirty seconds. We've been able to cut the radio budget by two-thirds by advertising salsa nights exclusively on the Web." That's about $1,000 per week. Martin was also able to quit printing and handing out flyers to promote events at the club.

When he gets more time, Martin hopes to add more entertainment to the site itself, such as live music shows or video
dance lessons. "We're small compared to other companies on
the Web," he says. But he figures being small is an advantage.
"We can do things pretty quickly."

The Online Help Desk

Some companies, like computer companies and those located in high-tech
areas, can already reach a large percentage of their customers online. Those
customers are already on the high-tech edge, comfortable with the Web, and
used to finding goods, services, and information there. For those companies,
it's easy to provide customers with support and service online. It's a model that
other lower-tech companies will be using more and more, as more consumers
get online and begin exploring ways to use the Web. The most famous example
of this kind of site is Federal Express's Web site. There, consumers can track
the routes of their packages after typing in the waybill number. Instead of calling Federal Express and probably waiting on hold to find out where the package is, consumers can quickly check for themselves. Federal Express is a large
low-tech company that's realized the advantage of this type of site. But smaller
companies can also set one up.

Say a customer has a broken garbage disposal—a pressing problem, but not
in need of an instant fix. The customer can visit the manufacturer's Web site
and read through a list of common disposal problems and their solutions. He
tries those fixes but they don't work, so he sends an email message to the support staff describing the problem. The manufacturer receives the email that
same day, perhaps within an hour, and immediately sends an email back telling
the customer that the problem is being researched. The support staffer checks
that customer's record and finds that the machine is still under warranty. After
troubleshooting his particular problem, the company sends a message back
suggesting a few more fixes he might try, along with a list of local approved
repair shops. The customer can then visit the repair shop Web sites and perhaps
even schedule a repair visit online. The customer is happy—he got a helpful
response the same day his disposal broke. The company is happy—they pay for
fewer phone lines since more customers are contacting them via the Web, and
they don't need as many support people since each person can handle more
email messages than phone calls.

At this point, online customer service only complements traditional phone
support because many customers are still more comfortable picking up a tele-

phone than navigating to a Web site. Phone support is also sometimes more immediate. A customer with a pressing problem can get a quick answer, as long as the hold time is short and phone support is available twenty-four hours a day. But increasing numbers of customers are happier sending email queries to a company. There aren't any frustrating voicemail levels to wade through, and the customer isn't sitting on hold, wasting time and getting angry. Instead, the customer sends the message quickly, knowing the company is working on the problem while he's doing something besides waiting on the phone.

Let's look at a business-to-business example. Say that a large automobile manufacturer has contracted with a small tool-and-die firm to produce molds for a part. During the development stage, the customer and company can communicate by leaving messages for each other at the Web site. Anyone involved in the process—engineers, designers, and salespeople—can read the stored email files detailing problems and solutions. The site can display design files, three-dimensional illustrations, material specifications, and contact information and schedules for all those involved in the process. All of those people can respond and interact easily, without playing telephone tag or sitting on hold.

This kind of site can be combined with other models. Perhaps the site also offers transactions, or maybe it's also a promotional site. The customer service section can bring in revenue, but only if the company charges for support. Then the same issues apply to charging for that support as apply to selling products or services online.

Any company with customers can begin using this model. If you suspect that few of your company's customers are online, don't dedicate an employee to online technical support at the beginning. Instead, have the person who gathers and forwards all of the site's email send all support questions to a phone support employee. That person can either contact the customer via telephone or write an email message to be forwarded by the Web site person. Once demand increases for online service, then dedicate staffers to that area.

CASE STUDY

Virtual Reality Labs:
Offering Customer Support Online

Online customer service is much more effective than phone service at Virtual Reality Labs, a science and entertainment

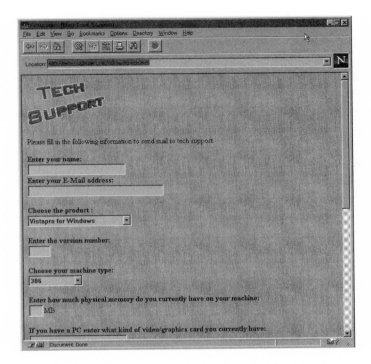

Virtual Reality Labs saves time and money by using this online form to process customer questions and complaints.

software publisher. "The more you can narrow it down in advance, the faster you can figure out what the problem is," says Tim Finer, technical director. The San Luis Obispo, California–based company created an online technical support area on their Web site, which went live in early 1995. By early 1996, the site was already handling about 30 percent of the $2 million company's customer service.

One of the company's technical support staffers had the idea to set up an online form for customers to fill out. On the telephones, support staffers have to walk through a script, probing for specific information, taking anywhere from a few to up to thirty minutes. On the Web, the needed information is sent instantly via email. A one-page form lets customers select options like the type of computer they're using, its configuration, and what error message they've received. When the customer is finished filling out the form, a click of the mouse emails it directly to Virtual Reality Labs' customer service department. "Using the form is much easier than making people navigate around on the Web site, then find our email spot and mail a question, filling in the details themselves." Rather than letting customers spell out the problem, the form walks them through the information technical support staffers need before beginning to research their problem. "In any kind of customer service, there's a lot of detail that people don't know they need to give you," Finer says. "And with email, you want to gather as much information up front so you aren't going back and forth."

Turnaround isn't quite as fast as phone support—a day or two for solutions online, but usually the same day via telephone. Finer thinks customers don't mind the longer solution time because their part of the transaction—sending the question—is not as time-consuming as waiting on the telephone. "The phone is a faster response, but email is more convenient." Processing eight to ten online queries a day takes the time of one of the four full-time support staffers.

In mid 1996, VRL decided to bring their previously outsourced Web site in house to implement order-entry and database search capabilities. Before the move, they paid about $45 per month for the Web site storage and maintenance, making changes and upgrades themselves. Storing the site in-house enables the company to add even more customer support services with quicker turnaround time.

The E-zine

One company executive describes most Web sites as being like mousetraps. The problem, he says, is that there's not enough cheese and too much trap. A magazine site tries to build a better mousetrap by offering lots of information that consumers are interested in, and downplaying the "trap," or the way those consumers earn income for the site. When done well, a magazine site offers consumers information they're interested in, without pushing them to make a purchase.

There are many examples of magazine sites on the Web. Most of them are companies that formed just to make money online. That's because those companies often have a better grasp of how to take advantage of this new medium than existing companies.

For example, say a small scuba diving retailer sets up a Web site. But instead of just listing equipment for sale and classes offered, the site follows the magazine model and on the first page lists several articles about training, travel tips, and vacation resorts. After the shop publicizes the site in newsgroups and in traditional advertising forums, people start checking in for the latest dive information. If the site merely offered products for sale, there would be no incentive to visit for those consumers who aren't currently in the market for equipment. But by offering industry information, the site draws anybody with a general interest in the subject. While at the site, a visitor might suddenly remember a need to purchase an extra underwater flashlight.

Or the visitor might not buy anything. But the fact that anyone visited at all still provides a revenue stream for the site, if the site documents that visit. Using tracking software (more about how this works in chapter 8), a company can monitor how many people visit the site and how long they stay. If the company asks visitors to register by filling out a short form, it gathers even more demographic information about those visitors. The scuba shop, for example, might have a form asking if the visitor is a certified scuba diver and at what level, what equipment they have, and how often they dive. That information can then be shown to advertisers, such as dive equipment manufacturers, to convince them to pay for an ad on the site. This is the same way that controlled-circulation magazines make money.

It's also a great way for Web sites to make money. Software makes it easy for visitors to register by typing responses into a form that can be emailed to the company that maintains the site. Software also easily tracks numbers of visitors to the site, so unlike magazines, companies with Web sites—even those who don't ask visitors to fill out forms—can prove how many "readers" they have.

Any company that can write articles or round up resources about their industry can create this kind of site, but for a site to be advertiser-sponsored, it's essential to determine which potential sponsors want to reach your customers but aren't direct competitors to you. A business-to-business environmental cleanup service could post articles on their site about hazardous waste, then sell ad space to environmental magazines, organizations, and companies that manufacture cleanup equipment, for example. A child-care center could write child development stories, then sell ad space to clothing manufacturers, baby food companies, and safety device and toy manufacturers. Avweb writes about airplane maintenance and operation, then sells ad space to pilot equipment manufacturers.

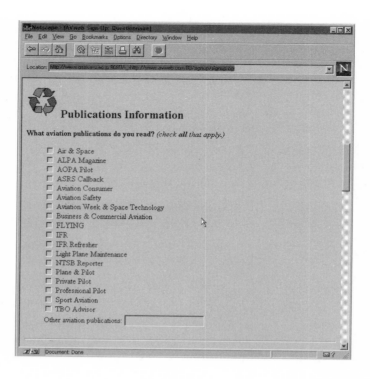

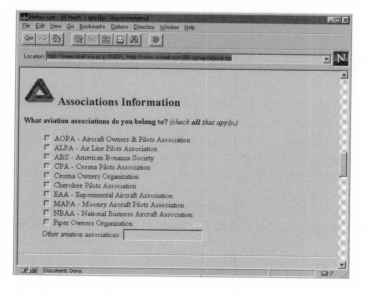

*Avweb generates advertising revenue at its magazine site by collecting
detailed demographics.*

CASE STUDY

Avweb: Attracting Readers and Selling Ads

"On the Web, most consumers aren't willing to pay for things," Carl Marbach believes. But he's convinced that advertisers are. By the end of 1995, Marbach's six-month-old Web site, Avweb, was already drawing revenues of a few thousand dollars per month from a total of twelve different advertisers and links to other aviation-related Web sites. By writing articles for pilots, Marbach draws enough qualified readers to the site to sell advertising and pointers, and he also plans to claim a percentage of his advertisers' online sales, eventually growing revenues to a six-figure range.

With a background in publishing trade magazines, Marbach has had experience with the publishing industry's controlled-circulation model: Subscriptions are handed out for free, but in return, subscribers must fill out a detailed form giving information about themselves. The magazine publisher then has more information about subscribers than a paid circulation publisher does, and uses those statistics to sell advertising, which pays the printing and circulation costs. Marbach applies the same model to Avweb. "Avweb is a magazine," he says. "It just happens to be published electronically instead of on paper."

Marbach chose this model because he believes that, eventually, all Web sites will be like his. "Most will migrate toward having some editorial content in order to attract people on a regular basis," he says. Some of those sites will also offer their own products for sale. Others will be advertiser-sponsored or offer the sponsor's products for sale—both of which apply to Avweb. Advertisers will want to know what they're getting for their money. "Not only can I tell you how many subscribers I have," Marbach says, "but I know who they are. I can give you more information than a print magazine can." Marbach says that his information gathered from registered visitors is more useful when dealing with advertisers than is traditional tracking software information. "If you're selling ads to Proctor and Gamble and you start talking about hit rates and domains, they'd look at you like you were from Mars. You need to talk in traditional terms, about people. It's much more meaningful."

At Avweb, visitors must fill out a one-page survey before they can access the site's table of contents and marketplace. Based on that survey, Marbach knows, for example, that 32 percent of his "readers" own their own airplanes. "That's important to an advertiser who sells something that needs to be installed in an airplane." As competition for Web advertisers heats up, this type of information will become increasingly important. "If you can't give it to advertisers, they'll go to a competitor who can." Other Web sites and industry publications are competing with Avweb for advertising dollars, but Marbach thinks there is still room for his company to make money. "Most successful markets have more than one publication. The advertiser gets twice the exposure advertising in more than one place."

Because it's published electronically, Avweb can offer consumers interesting elements that a print magazine can't, such as live discussion groups, instant email to editors and writers, and easily accessible archived stories from previous issues. It's also updated more frequently than a print magazine, Marbach says—often weekly. "We have no publishing schedules, no deadlines, and no copy fitting problems." Marbach can run as many articles as he wants and cover breaking news stories that magazines normally leave to newspapers. Although some Web regulars might argue that his site is a little text-heavy, Marbach is taking advantage of the fact that his publishing costs are much lower than if he had to buy paper and mail it out. "If I have 100,000 readers instead of 30,000 readers, my costs don't go up at all." Marbach serves the site in-house, using a Digital Equipment ALPHAserver 1000 with 160 megabytes of memory and 10 gigabytes of disk space, connected to a T1 phone line. The computer runs UNIX 3.0 operating system, with the Netscape Secure Commerce Server.

The site opened in July 1995 with about ten advertisers. Marbach expects to increase his revenue stream from his advertisers once they begin offering products for sale at his site. "The foremost goal in publishing on the Web is building traffic," he says. As that traffic increases, Marbach will have enough muscle to ask advertisers for commissions on their sales. Unlike with a print magazine, Avweb's software can easily track when a customer makes an online purchase from one of the magazine's advertisers in the store section of the site. Since the magazine can demonstrate that they brought that customer to the advertiser, they can claim a percentage of the sale. Marbach also charges $500 per month for links to other aviation sites. Avweb offers visitors an internal search engine that sorts through advertisements by keyword, which creates another revenue source. Marbach can charge classified advertisers to list their ads in the search engine, so that consumers can type in "Cessna" and find all Cessna aircraft for sale.

"The barrier to entry to creating a Web site is fairly small," Marbach says. "The difference between sites is that some are properly capitalized and run as proper businesses sticking it out for the long term." Following some type of successful business model is key, he says. "Just putting something up on the Web isn't good enough."

The Internal Site

Not all successful Web sites are actually on the Web. Large companies with many different office locations have for some time been using internal Web sites—known as intranet sites—to give employees one central location for company information. Now small companies are picking up on the benefits of having an in-house computer dedicated to storing general data like employee handbooks, policy statements, project timelines, internal job postings, and staffing announcements. Obviously, this is information that companies don't want widely available on the Web, but by setting up a site on an internal computer that's not connected to any Internet phone lines, employees can access it whenever they want to, just like consumers visit Web sites. Using Web software to set it up means that it's easy to maintain and easy for employees to navigate using a point-and-click browser.

This kind of site doesn't make sales. In fact, it doesn't communicate with customers at all. But it can save the company money. Say an employee needs to check on the company vacation policy. Normally someone would have to dig through a file and find the information, then copy it for the employee. With an intranet site, the employee gets the information quickly, without the increased labor costs. Or say a company is working on developing a new product—a new ice cream flavor, for example. Using the intranet site to track the project means anyone associated with it can instantly get an update on its progress. Instead of waiting for scheduled meetings to learn where the flavoring is sourced, which markets are likely to carry the new flavor, and who's designing the package, employees can get daily updates from the internal Web site. The person in charge of scheduling the taste-testing will know immediately when a prototype is ready, instead of waiting for a meeting.

In a tiny office with few employees, this kind of site might seem like overkill. With only a few employees working closely together, everyone is likely to be communicating regularly enough to stay updated on projects. The company probably hasn't even developed an employee handbook yet. But once companies like that begin to grow, communications can deteriorate quickly. New hires join, and increased sales bring on new projects and customers. Pretty soon, nobody knows what's going on or even who to ask. Setting up this kind of site early on can put responsibility on the site, instead of an overworked CEO or manager, to keep employees informed.

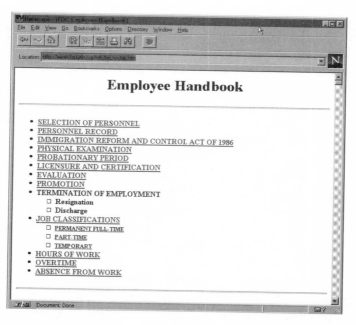

In this simple internal, or intranet, site, Forsyth Dental Center stores important company information for employees to access.

CASE STUDY

Forsyth Dental Center: Intranetting for Employees

Boston-based Forsyth Dental Center was decentralized and disorganized. "The staff has always worked in entrepreneurial fashion," says David Hanson, director of computing and network technology at the small nonprofit agency. Historically, the organization had been staffed with various researchers, students, administrators, and support technicians, most working independently. The result was a lack of central communication and information exchange. The solution? An internal Web page where corporate information is stored. "There's been a lack of good record-keeping in this institution," Hanson says. "When people couldn't find information, they just let it slip. Now that's become less of a problem."

Hanson wanted to set up a type of virtual lab notebook—a computer where everyone in the organization could store and access company research data. At the time, Lotus Notes was the only software package that would fill Hanson's needs, but it was also prohibitively expensive for the cash-strapped nonprofit. "Given the size of our organization and our resources, we just couldn't do it," he says. He put his plans on hold.

Then in late 1995, after finally securing company Internet access and networking Forsyth's internal computers to one another, Hanson realized that an internal Web site could meet his needs. "It started as people needing access to documents like the employee handbook," he says. "The CEO suggested we put it on our Web site. Since we didn't want things like that on the external site, we figured we'd start an internal site." Hanson bought a Dell Optiplex XMT 5100 with 32 megabytes of RAM and a one-gigabyte hard drive for $6,000. Vermeer's Front Page Web development software was $300. For the operating system software, Hanson added another site license for Windows NT for $400.

The site went live at the end of the year and now stores the company's handbook, various administrative reports, and safety and chemical hygiene policies. "There were electronic copies of all of that somewhere," he says. "I just had to dig them up and do some minor editing." He hasn't had a chance yet to add the virtual lab notebook section of the internal site. "We're very small," Hanson says of the computer staff for the 125-person organization. "There are only two of us who run the network and operate all the Web stuff." To help out, he's asked a few staffers to create sections on the Web site for their departments.

The internal site makes information more accessible. "Finding stuff in paper files isn't easy, especially when there's a lot of it," he says. "Before, it just wasn't readily available. Now you just fire up Netscape and click on the policies." Staffers have mentioned the difference, Hanson says. "I've had people tell me that before, they never bothered to look things up. But now when they have questions or concerns, they can click on their desktop."

What each of these companies has learned is how to attract people to their Web sites. They've each pinpointed something their company offers that draws visitors, whether those are customers, potential customers or employees. Some are able to make money directly from the site; others cut expenses by using a Web site to streamline certain operations. Unless a company is able to focus the site to offer something of interest, that expensive online investment won't have any return. Next, we'll look at different ways companies can promote that interesting site, so that everybody on the Internet knows about it, visits and makes it work the way it's intended.

7

• •

Do Drop In: Publicizing the Site and Attracting Visitors

Smart companies set goals in their business plans and marketing strategies. Say a catalog company rents a particular mailing list. The company hopes for a 3 percent return on the highly-qualified, expensive list. If the list doesn't deliver the desired return on their investment, the company won't make the same bad investment twice. Every company should do the same thing with its Web page. Once the costs of setting up a site are known, it's time to establish a hoped-for return. There are three elements to setting a goal for the Web site: What kind of return is desired? How will it be measured? And over what time period?

The type of return doesn't have to be just financial, in the form of a certain percentage of total sales by a particular date. It could be to gather a certain number of names for a mailing list, or to cut company mailing or telephone expenses by a certain amount after handing over some customer service functions to the Web site. Perhaps the company hopes to cut marketing expenses, while still posting the same sales growth percentages. Whatever it is, the return should be set up to measure whatever is the main focus of the Web site. For example, you probably wouldn't want to focus on hiring a certain percentage of employees from Web site applications if it's a catalog site. It would be more to the point to measure sales instead. In the beginning, choose one main aspect to measure. If that goes well, it's easy enough to add more areas to evaluate later.

Once the type of return is established, make sure there is a way to measure it and that systems are in place to do it. Web sales can easily be measured at a site that handles online transactions. But how would you measure the portion of decreased mailing expenses attributable to the Web site? How would you decide if customer service functions are successful on the Web (perhaps by looking for decreased telephone costs, or a certain number of existing customers signing up for online support packages)? It's important to take the time up front to establish clear guidelines for measuring the site's success or failure, so that there can be no question once the site goes live. (Chapter 8 discusses how to measure traffic at a Web site.)

When the site opens, that's when it's time to start measuring how well it's doing. But when to stop? Some companies consider a Web site to be a long-term investment, worth sticking with for several years before evaluating whether it's a success or failure. Others can't afford to funnel funds into a non-money-making endeavor for more than a few months. Whatever the time frame, be realistic. It's unlikely that any Web site will be pulling down 50 percent of a company's sales in a few months. Talk to other companies who have had sites up for a while, and ask how they evaluate their sites.

Online Promotions

The key to any site's success or failure is traffic. No company can make sales, advertise, offer customer service, or charge advertisers unless people visit the Web site, and they don't necessarily come just because you build it. The site has to be promoted, so Web users can find it among the increasing number of sites out there. This doesn't mean launching a high-powered and expensive ad campaign. One of the great advantages of the Web for small businesses is that it's inexpensive—often free—to let people know that a site is open and where it is. These are the best ways to get the word out after opening a Web site:

Email advertisements: Most email programs allow users to create little files of text that automatically append to the bottom of all email messages. So every time a CEO sends an email message, at the end it might say something like, "XYZ Company, meeting your real estate needs since 1944." The file is called a "signature file," and any company with a Web site should include the URL and a brief description of the site in key employees' signature file. Thus, every email sent could also include a brief ad like, "Visit our Web site at *www. newproperty.com* to play Land on Boardwalk!"

The key to an effective signature file is to keep it short, ideally four lines or fewer. Some people create very elaborate signature files, drawing little pictures or quoting long passages from books or poems. This type of file just takes up space, and nobody bothers to read the whole thing after the first time. But a short file usually gets at least glanced at every time, flashing quickly in front of people and prompting them to remember the message.

Direct email: If your company's site is set up to collect email addresses of visitors, add a question next to that section asking if they'd mind receiving email notifying them of changes to your Web site, or changes in the industry, or changes and updates to whatever key information your site offers. Once armed with a list of users willing to receive email, start sending it to them. Don't abuse their trust by overwhelming them with press releases every time a minor change is made to the site, but do put together a regular mailer, perhaps once a month, pointing out a few new products available on the site or key issues discussed there. This mailer shouldn't steal the site's thunder. It should be more of a tease designed to make readers want to visit the site. Keep it very short and current. (For more details on how one company leverages its electronic mailing list, read about Alberto's Nightclub in chapter 6.)

Online billboards: A collection of Internet discussion groups, known as "newsgroups," works like bulletin boards—people can post messages on certain topics. Anyone who visits the newsgroup can read all of the past messages and also post messages themselves. There are more than 16,000 newsgroups, each one focusing on a specific topic, such as pet health care, foreign car repair, Web page development, computers for sale, or fan clubs for rock musicians. This area of the Internet is notoriously noncommercial, and users hate posted advertisements. When two Arizona lawyers posted a message to all of the newsgroups advertising their green card services a few years ago, so many newsgroup readers sent them hate mail that their ISP couldn't process all of the email and had to shut down for several days. Despite this, some companies do market to the newsgroups successfully.

The first essential tactic is to focus on newsgroups only where your company's product or service is of interest. Albert Martin of Alberto's Nightclub posts messages in alternative and Latin music newsgroups, for example, not just in any newsgroup where he thinks the majority of readers are in his target demographic. The second thing to remember is to read the messages posted there for several weeks before posting your own. Perhaps that particular group is violently opposed to any marketing, no matter how soft-pedaled—it's better to learn that before posting a message than after. Third, post very brief messages, making clear in the subject line of the message what the topic is. For example, listing the subject as "Great opportunity to save!" marks that message clearly as an advertisement, begging for angry email in response. But listing "Info on new nonstick cookware" makes the subject clear. Those who don't want to know about the cookware won't read the message, and therefore won't respond with angry email.

Fourth, be honest about who you are—someone from a company trying to sell a product or service. Writing "I work for a company that sells Sheep Brand Soap, and here's how to reach us if you're interested" will be more respected in the newsgroups than writing "I've used Sheep Brand Soap and love it. Email me if you'd like to know more." And keep those messages short and sweet, avoiding hyperbole. Since many users are paying by the hour to access the Internet, they don't like to waste time online. Some companies first post messages in the target newsgroups, asking if the participants would mind their messages. For example, in a sports newsgroup a company might post a message saying, "Would people here be interested in occasional information on new shoe technology?" Often, many users are and will respect a company for asking.

CASE STUDY

Lasermax: Promoting in Newsgroups

It was a customer who told William Houde-Smith that his company's product was a hot topic in one of the Internet's newsgroups. A police officer called to place an order for Lasermax's gun laser sights and happened to mention that he'd found out about the product after posting a question about it in a newsgroup about guns. The day after his post, the customer had received more than eighty messages about the Rochester, New York–based company.

Houde-Smith knew this was a forum that he had to explore. "I bought a book on the Internet, and in ten minutes I was up and running." He started reading the messages that were posted in the newsgroups that his customer had recommended. In one message, a person asked how one of Lasermax's products worked. "I posted a non-hype kind of response," he says. "I knew enough Internet etiquette so I didn't flog the product. I focused on the product concept and ideas."

```
u  897   -  rec.antiques                              Discussing
u  898   -  alt.folklore.science                      The folklor
u  899   -  alt.sci.physics.acoustics                 The soundne
u  900   -  alt.3d                                    Three-dimen
u  901   -  comp.sys.mac.databases                    Database sy
u  902   -  sci.astro.hubble                          Processing
u  903   -  alt.pcnews
u  904   -  alt.rave                                  Techno-cult
u  905   -  alt.sport.bowling                         In the gutt
u  906   -  alt.tv.mst3k                              Hey, you ro
u  907   -  alt.tv.simpsons.itchy-scratchy
u  908   -  alt.tv.ren-n-stimpy                       Some change
u  909   -  alt.fan.pratchett                         For fans of
u  910   -  un.comp-iss
u  911   -  alt.cad                                   Computer Ai
u  912   -  alt.fan.tom-robbins                       31 flavours

   <n>=set current to n, TAB=next unread, /=search pattern, c)atchup,
   g)oto, j=line down, k=line up, h)elp, m)ove, q)uit, r=toggle all/unread,
   s)ubscribe, S)ub pattern, u)nsubscribe, U)nsub pattern, y)ank in/out
```

Usenet is a popular discussion area on the Internet. Each of these list-
ings is a newsgroup filled with messages about a particular topic.

"I was amazed about the discussions about our products," he says. "There are a lot of philosophical issues among people who use our sights." Houde-Smith makes clear that he's from Laser-max, but he says it doesn't bother people in the newsgroup that he has a commercial interest. "They enjoy the fact that I'm an industry expert."

The group Houde-Smith regularly visits has a resource section that lists Lasermax's Web site URL. He says it helps the $5 million company to have someone regularly monitoring the newsgroups and contributing to discussions there. "The newsgroups are sort of like fishing nets that direct people to the Web site."

Search engine keywords: As noted in chapter 2, most Web users rely on the big search engines to find sites. A person looking for information on children's educational toys isn't usually going to check the newsgroups for messages or look through magazine advertisements for Web page URLs listed in the ad. Instead, that person will log on to the Web, then go to a search engine like

InfoSeek or Yahoo! and type in "children's toys" or "educational toys" and see what sites come up. Clicking on the link takes the person to those sites. If your company site wants to get a piece of most of the Web's traffic, being listed with the search engines is a must.

The search engines ask for a list of keywords when companies register their sites. Whether your company is designing an in-house site or outsourcing the work, you'll need to come up with a list of keywords. Companies do try to use tricks to make sure their site will be first on the list. For example, a travel agent might list "travel" as a keyword thirty times. When a user searches on "travel," that site will come up first because it matches the criteria more than a site that only has "travel" as a keyword once or even fifteen times. Some search engines have already written software programs to ignore repeating keywords, so this trick isn't as effective as it once was. Another trick many developers use is to embed profane words in the keyword section of the site. That way, the site appears when users search on those words, which happens a lot. Unfortunately, this tactic doesn't pay off because Web users get angry when they click on sites that don't deliver on the subject matter of the keyword hit.

Listing with most search engines is a free service. At each search engine site is a "list your site" or "register" button. Clicking on this starts an easy registration process for listing a site. If your company doesn't register, most of the search engines will find it eventually anyway and list it (they have software programs that scour the Web periodically for new sites), but why wait? There are also free services, such as Submit It! at submit-it.perma-link.com/submit-it/, that will list sites with the search engines. Some search engines, like Yahoo!, have editors who review sites and decide whether or not to include them in their listings. To be included on Yahoo!, a site has to offer Web users some value.

CASE STUDY

PhotoCollect: Listing with the Search Engines

Allen Klotz debuted his photography gallery's Web site in August 1995, but PhotoCollect didn't list with the search engines until October. "Yahoo! wasn't going to review us more than once, so we wanted to be absolutely ready," he says. If his site weren't completely ready or didn't impress Yahoo!'s editors, he would have missed his chance to be listed there.

Klotz also listed his New York–based gallery's site with other search engines, including InfoSeek, the only one that asked him for a fee. "We didn't pay it," he says. "They didn't enforce it." There are so many search engines on the Web right now that it's likely that InfoSeek would just shrink its own listings if it started insisting on fees.

To list on each search engine, Klotz visited their Web sites and filled out a quick online form. Each registration took about a minute, and Glotz selected his own keywords to classify his site. Afterward, he tested a few by searching on his chosen keywords and wasn't pleased by what he found. "If you type in 'PhotoCollect' as a keyword, it finds us immediately," he says. "But if you type in 'photography' it brings up thousands of entries, and that's not very much help to us. Is someone really going to look through thousands of entries, or just click on the first one and then leave the list?" That's the problem many companies face, and the reason that Web developers are always trying tricks to make sure their clients' sites pop up first on searches by common keywords.

"I'd advise companies to list with the search engines," he says. "They have to." Not listing with a search engine is equivalent to opening a store but not listing in the business yellow pages. "Just be aware that they're slow and overworked. It's hard for them to keep up with the Web's growth." So far, Klotz says, his site has been very successful, and he did make it into Yahoo!'s listings. "We've sold expensive things, which is a shock. We've sold prints for up to $4,000, which is a lot of money. Plus we're currently tracking down prints for about twenty-five hot leads."

Traditional advertising: Don't overlook other, more traditional marketing materials that can contribute to awareness of a Web site. Include the URL on everything that goes outside the company, including business cards, print media advertisements, direct mail pieces, trade show brochures, even television advertising. By doing this, both current customers and prospects can be directed to the site. And seeing a URL in print instantly grabs the attention of people who are already on the Web but have yet to see your company's site.

CASE STUDY

Cattron: Using Traditional Marketing

"Lately we've really come on strong, making sure our Web address is on everything," says Nora Songer, marketing director at Cattron, a small industrial equipment manufacturer in Charlottesville, Pennsylvania. Cattron has had a promotional Web site since late 1994. After the push to include the site's URL on all printed material, the company noticed a corresponding boost in traffic. "A lot of our vendors are suprised and pleased by it," says Songer. "They think it's incredible that this small company in West Pennsylvania is on the Web."

The company sends out 10,000 pieces of direct mail each year and buys half a dozen space ads in trade journals each month. Along with traditional information like phone and fax numbers, the company's URL goes on every one of those ads and mailers. It's also on every employee's business card and is featured in the company's listing in various in buyers' guides.

A potential buyer might not go to the trouble to fill in a direct mail response card, Songer figures. But that same person browsing the Web later might remember that Cattron has a Web site. "They can go on and not worry about having to answer a bunch of survey questions or being interviewed over the phone," she says, citing reasons why many potential customers don't call or return mailers to companies for information.

Another reason Cattron publicizes their company URL is for international customers. "Our offices are only open from eight A.M. to five P.M. That means someone on the West Coast is not going to be able to contact us at five P.M. their time," she says. "But if they have a question, they can look at our Web site and send us email. We've had people from Europe and the Far East look at products on our Web site. During their business hours, they can get the information they want."

Songer realized that linking the Web site with traditional forms of advertising is important because each medium attracts a different type of buyer. "I think most people right now still prefer magazines—the printed word that they can hold and touch," she says. "But a whole new generation has grown up with computers, and they'll be making buying decisions too."

The best address: Every Web site should strive to get an address, or URL, that's easy for customers to remember. This address is determined by registering the computer that stores the Web site with InterNIC, the organization that hands out computer names. This name tells the user's computer where to look for the site's computer. Companies that aren't careful can end up with a confusing string of characters, like "www.znet/~iStore.frodonet.com/W3.html." But that same company can usually have "www.ourcompany.com," if it's registered with InterNIC. These are also known as "domains" or "domain names."

It's becoming increasingly difficult for a company to register its first choice of domain name, because it may already be taken by another company. For example, a cleaning service called Minute Maid may find that a fruit juice site has already registered "www.minutemaid.com" and a laundry service has already grabbed "www.clean.com." So make a list of choices in case the first few aren't available. Because of this, it's best to register the domain as soon as possible when creating an online strategy. It can sometimes take months before InterNIC responds to registration requests—by 1996 they were already processing more than one request per minute.

Any service provider or Web developer can register a domain for its clients. For a company handling registration in-house, third-party services can register domains (see the appendix). Anyone can contact InterNIC directly at their Web site (rs.internic.net/rs-internic.html) and follow the online registration prompts. (More on registering domains in chapter 4.)

CASE STUDY

Sonnet Software: Making Second Choice Work

"We knew the domain we wanted and put it on the registration application," says Shawn Carpenter, sales and marketing director at Sonnet Software. The $2 million Liverpool, New York–based company assumed they'd be able to register "sonnet.com" with InterNIC. They assumed wrong.

Doug Bray, a technical staffer, asked Sonnet's service provider how to file for the domain. They offered to handle it for him. "Normally they charge fifty dollars for it," he says. "But since we signed a few years' contract with them, they waived it." A representative at the ISP—Dreamscape, located in Syracuse—did a quick search while Bray was on the telephone and saw that Sonnet was already taken. Bray was surprised and frustrated. "We had to go back to the drawing board to think of new names," he says.

A few days later, armed with several options, Bray tried again. The company's second choice, "sonnetusa.com" wasn't taken, so Dreamscape quickly filed the paperwork. In two weeks, Sonnet was officially awarded the new domain.

To help promote their online presence and build awareness of the somewhat awkward URL, Sonnet printed up special business cards. They list information for "Sonnet Online," including the company email address, Web site URL, and traditional company address and phone number. Carpenter says that getting the word out immediately helped publicize the domain name. "We took the cards right away to our first major trade show, and we got a lot of hits after that." Carpenter admits that it probably hurts Sonnet to not have "sonnet.com" as a domain. "I know some customers have taken a guess at our email address and sent questions to 'sonnet.com,' " he says. But the business cards have made a difference. "Once someone contacts us a first time, the name sticks in their heads."

A software company like Sonnet can pretty much assume that the majority of its customers are familiar with the Web and probably already have Internet accounts, so promoting their site is likely to pay off quickly. But what about lower-tech companies? What if most people in their industry, including suppliers, competitors, and customers, aren't using the Web? Why bother to promote a site when it's likely to have little return? Companies in that position have two choices. The first is to publicize the company's URL anyway and be the industry leader. Companies that do this will have time on their side—they'll be able to work with their Web site and hone it, making mistakes and moving on before the rest of the industry catches up.

The second option is to drag customers online with the company. CompuServe's Internet division, Spry, offers a computer disk with a customizable version of Mosaic's Web browser. Pricing varies according to the order, but it isn't cheap. Basically, a company orders pre-programmed computer disks. The firm can then hand disks out to its customers or suppliers as a premium. The person who gets the disk just pops it into a computer, then it automatically dials a preprogrammed Internet service provider and loads the company's Web site. That's one more person on the Web and one more person at the company's Web site.

Paying for Pointers

Listing a Web site on the search engines ensures that that site's address will pop up each time a search finds its keyword. Then Web users click on the address and jump instantly to that site. This is a common way of using pointers, or hypertext links. Links are the best way to use the Web itself to promote a site because that's how Web users navigate. The most likely way they'll find new sites is by clicking around. Because of this, it's important to make smart use of the places you point visitors to and the ones that bring visitors to you.

When companies talk about *paying* for links, they're talking about links that point Web users only in the direction of their site. Links do work both ways—they bring visitors to a site and also send visitors away. But nobody pays to send visitors away. Most companies don't really care which sites are sending visitors to them by linking to their site. What they really care about is where their links send their visitors. That's when negotiations get tricky.

In 1996, there were still no guidelines on paying for pointers, just as there weren't any for pricing Web developers and servers. It would be simple if there were standards based on the number of visitors sent via each pointer—for example, every ten thousand users that one site sends another would cost a thousand dollars—but no such guidelines exist. Companies simply charge what they think that the market will bear. Some charge by the number of visitors the link actually sends, some charge by the amount of traffic their site has, and some just charge a flat monthly fee for a link. A popular site like Playboy might charge more than $20,000 per month for a link from their site to, say, a small clothing catalog site. But another company might just ask the catalog to put in a link to their site in return and pay nothing. Part of the reason that there are no pricing standards is that this new industry hasn't yet settled down. Only in 1995 did software tools begin to emerge that accurately track the number of people who visit sites. Before this type of accurate information became available, it was difficult to establish any sort of pricing standards.

If a company's tracking reports aren't convincing enough to pay for a pointer, consider offering to trade links. This is a budget approach that many small companies take. Basically, it's like saying, "I'll point to your site if you'll point to mine." Sometimes pointers just aren't worth buying, but they are almost always worth having.

Paying for Advertisements

Paying for advertisements is different than paying for pointers. The big search engines will all point to a company site for free, but if a company wants to buy an advertisement on the search engine's site, that costs much more than just a link. The advertisement is basically a glorified pointer. Many sites sell advertisements, but we'll use a popular search engine as an example. Say Joe's Microbrewery wants to buy an ad on Lycos's search engine site. Joe designs a small graphic ad that will stretch across the computer screen. Lycos takes the ad and makes it a pointer or a link, so that when Web users click on that link, it takes them directly to Joe's Web site. Whenever Web users visit Lycos to do a keyword search, a different advertisement appears on the screen, and sometimes that ad is Joe's. Joe pays Lycos about $6,000 per month. In return, Lycos guarantees 200,000 impressions during that month. In early 1996, Lycos was offering about seven different advertising packages, and this was one of the least expensive.

The search engines aren't the only sites charging for advertisements. Web sites with a lot of traffic also charge, and so do the online services. But before any company pays for an advertisement or link, it's essential to ask for and carefully review tracking report information from the company charging for the ad or pointer (more in chapter 8). Unfortunately, those reports are sometimes confidential. If so, ask for client referrals, and ask those companies what kind of traffic was directed to their site from the ad or pointer. Was it worth it? If it didn't pay off for them, it might not for you. Don't be afraid to play hardball in negotiating prices for pointers—not much is set in stone. But don't be surprised if the company you're negotiating with turns your offer down cold. They may feel that there are a million other fish in the sea who will pay their prices, and they're probably right.

The Ratio of External to Internal Links

There are links that send Web users to other sites, known as external links, and then there are links that send users to another page within the same site, called internal links. It's easy to get carried away with links, pointing Web users to all kinds of interesting sites. That's really one of the best things about the Web— it's easy for users to go where they like whenever they like by using pointers. But remember, external pointers send visitors *away* from the site to somewhere else on the Web, and they're likely to keep pushing forward instead of returning to the original site. Therefore it's important to keep a good ratio of external to internal links—a rough guideline followed by many designers is 80 percent internal to 20 percent external.

One trick that Web developers use is to program a short warning message to flash on the computer screen when users click on an external link. That message might say something like, "You're leaving our site now. Save the URL so you can come back easily." Users can then choose to save the Web site address in their browser software's memory by just pulling down the "save" option on the menu bar. This is called "bookmarking," and it saves users from having to remember long, awkward URLs of the sites they visit often. Instead, they just select a site from the bookmarked list on the browser, and the software remembers the URL. Another trick Web developers use to keep visitors within a particular site is to bury external links deep into a site, so that users must spend some there before they click on links to leave.

The Essentials for Any Site

Once users find a site—through a search engine, by reading a URL in a magazine ad, or by being sent to the site from a link on another site—there are certain things they'll expect to see no matter what. Ignoring these important elements will mark any site as amateurish and not worth visiting again:

It delivers what it promises: Say a Web user types "car repair" into a search engine, and Auto Mile Car Dealership turns up among the sites that list "car repair" in their keyword sections. That site had better have more than just a line reading, "Our repair shop is open ten hours a day" to justify listing "repair" in the keyword section. Otherwise, that user will be angry to have wasted the time visiting the site, only to learn there's no information on car repair there. Make sure that a keyword leads a user to a sizable amount of information at your site about that topic.

It doesn't take long to download: The classic mistake that many companies make is to include a large photo or sound or video clip on the Web site. Often

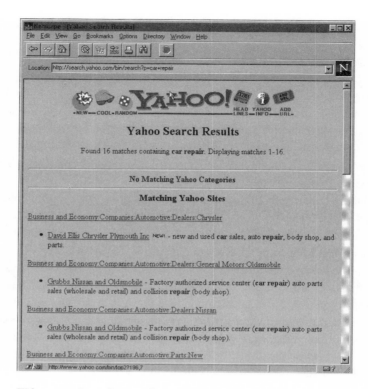

Web users rely on the search engines to find sites that have the information they want. By clicking on one of these listings, the user can go directly to that site.

it is of the CEO, who is saying something useless like, "Welcome to our Web site, we hope you like it." The problem is, graphics and sound take a really long time to download compared to text. For a Web user with a 14.4 modem, waiting four minutes for something that boring is bound to make them run away from the site. Many interesting visual effects can be created on Web sites that don't take long to download. For example, skinny horizontal graphics that stretch across the screen take shorter time to download than large ones that use a lot of vertical space. Black-and-white graphics load faster than color ones. Ask the Web developer what types of "low-bandwidth design" options could work for your site. If you're designing in-house, look through resources on Web design for low-bandwidth options (see appendix for design resources).

Company information is easy to find: On the Web, it doesn't matter if a company is in Missouri or Manitoba. With a click of the mouse, it's just as easy for Web users to reach one as it is the other. But nobody is living completely in cyberspace yet. Users want to know where the companies are in the real world.

Perhaps the customer lives near the company and would like to visit, or maybe they'd just find it interesting to know that a cactus greenhouse is located in Wisconsin. It's essential to place the Web site somewhere in traditional real-world space, so always list a physical company location. Even more essential is to include an address, as well as phone and fax numbers. Believe it or not, some Web users want to pick up the telephone and call a company, or mail in an order rather than email it. Usually this information provides reassurance that the site belongs to a real company and not a con artist. Sometimes the Web user just wants the information because he or she is more comfortable with traditional contact methods.

It's updated frequently: Most Web developers or in-house Web site adminis-trators update their sites at least once a week. This time-intensive task con-sumes a lot of labor, especially when the One-Hour Browse Rule is factored

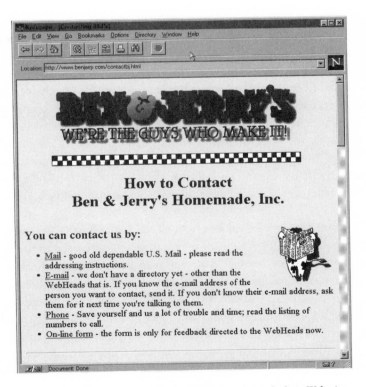

Although many users will contact companies through their Web sites, some will want traditional company information, like phone numbers and addresses.

into the equation: For every change made to the site, the person making the change should browse the Web for at least one hour. Keeping the site updated and refreshed is key for companies that expect visitors to return. There is so much action on the Web that it's tempting for visitors to jump somewhere more exciting if your company's site bores them.

There's some user interaction: One of the big advantages of this medium is that it allows users to interact immediately. They can send email, fill out a form, enter a contest, or request information the instant they have the urge. And they expect to be asked—it's part of the fun and entertainment of browsing the Web. A site with no "user feedback" email forms, no games to play, or no forms to fill out is a site counting the days before it dies.

One kind of interactive element some sites can include is a piece of software that will search a product database by keyword. For example, customers at a bicycle retailer Web site can type in "mountain bike locks" to get a list of the desired products. This internal search engine saves time compared to browsing an entire list of products or even the list of all bicycle locks. Customers appreciate that and are more likely to revisit that site rather than other bicycle retailer sites.

Another interactive and time saving piece of software is an online form. Like Virtual Reality Labs' customer service form profiled in chapter 6, these online forms can save time for the company and Web user. They can be used by visitors requesting company or product information, registering to visit the site, asking for specific customer service, or signing up for a customized email newsletter. They can even be structured so that the Web user can customize the page itself. By expressing preferences in an online form, the user can specify which parts of the Web site will show and which will be hidden on the next visit.

Web sites have copied another part of the Internet—the live "chat." On some Web sites, visitors can click on a button to go to a screen, or "room," where there is a list of the other visitors who are present at the same time. Anytime someone types a sentence and hits the "enter" key on the keyboard, everyone in the "chat room" instantly sees that person's name and the message and can respond. It's sort of like going to a small cocktail party, except everyone types instead of talks. It can be difficult to draw visitors regularly to these chat areas, and what frequently happens is someone will go into one but nobody else is there, so the visitor quickly leaves. The smart approach is to schedule discussions on specific topics and then publicize them, so that enough people attend at the same time to be able to carry on a conversation.

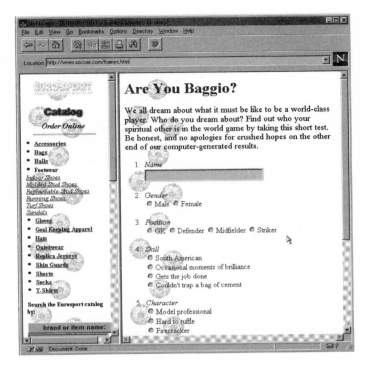

Short interactive games like this one at Eurosport's site keep Web users returning again and again.

CASE STUDY

Eurosport: Attracting Visitors

"We were looking for interactive things to put on the site," says Dave Wolf, new media director at Eurosport, a Hillsborough, North Carolina–based company. The $23 million soccer equipment cataloger had always strived to create interesting copy in their print catalog to draw readers. When they set up a Web site in the fall of 1995, they wanted to do the same.

What they came up with was an interactive feature called "Are You Baggio?" named for Roberto Baggio, one of the world's best soccer players. The feature works like this: Visitors fill out a seven-question survey, selecting their position, temperament, and skill level in the game of soccer. Then they click on a button, and a moment later a screen pops up with a photo and short essay about the professional soccer player that best matches the visitor's profile. Truly bad players are matched with a Eurosport manager. "It's definitely drawing people to the site," Wolf says. "That's what visitors are hitting the most." Eurosport's service provider, Catalogue.com, tells them that most of the site's two thousand-plus daily visitors are coming to the site from searching on famous soccer players' names on the search engines. Because their interest in famous soccer players drew them to the site, a game like "Are You Baggio?" is likely to appeal to those visitors.

Visitors who go to the Baggio feature from the home page must scroll down past a few articles about products and soccer players, and they must go past pages that offer to point them to the product catalog. Thus, Wolf has created a flow through his site, much like some retail stores that put the most popular items in the back of the store. When Wolf created the Baggio feature, he wanted it to be fairly involved, with many descriptive fields and perhaps some humorous quotes. But he was under deadline pressure to have it ready in time for the Web site's debut, so the feature stayed fairly simple. "Now I think that's a good thing," he says. Visitors, even those with slow modems, can play the little game quickly without waiting a long time for it to match them to a famous player. A quick feature like that will draw visitors back to the site again and again.

Whether or not to include some elements in a Web site is still being debated. For example, should a Web site be debuted before it's really finished? At an unfinished site, users who click on the unfinished section see a little "under construction" sign. The Web is filled with these. Some Web users hate it and won't return to a site that's under construction, especially if they do revisit once and it's *still* under construction. But evidently some users don't seem to mind. "Under construction" sites do still receive visitors. Some Web developers claim it can be a smart marketing move because it piques the interest of visitors, who figure that an unfinished Web site is worth revisiting to see how it turns out. For companies that decide to gamble on rolling out an unfinished site, there are two rules to follow for it to work: First, *most* of the site must be finished. Second, put a date on the unfinished section so visitors know when to expect completion. Otherwise, after returning several times to an "under construction" site that shows no signs of ever being finished, they'll give up.

■　　■　　■

A clever site will attract visitors, who will return regularly to see what's new. While they're browsing the site, they may also buy something. But if there is no sale, how does your company know that anyone has stopped by? It's not as if it's a real store, where the proprietor can see at any given moment how many customers have come in. No, in fact, it's better than that—Web site operators can collect more information than store owners can. How many people stop in during any given time period? Where do they come from, how long do they stay, and what do they look at? In chapter 8, we explain the many different ways that a company can track all of that information.

8

● ●

Hit Me!: Tracking Visitors

A company sets up a good-looking Web site, following all the tips and tricks for getting visitors to come early and often. The company hopes to build an electronic mailing list and to make sales to a certain percentage of the visitors. But how will the company gather those email addresses? And how will it know what part of the site visitors find the most interesting? Or which part compels visitors to make a purchase? One wonderful thing about the Web is that simple software programs exist to gather all of this information.

When advertising in traditional media, it's often impossible to accurately track customer response. When Bob's Cigar Shop takes out an advertisement in the local newspaper, nobody knows how many readers actually look at that ad or for how long. If Bob pesters every single walk-in customer, asking where they learned about his shop, he'll only get a rough idea of how many are making purchases based on his ad. If Bob wants to analyze his ad statistically, he'll have to invest a lot of time calculating how many readers the newspaper says it has, how many customers said they made a purchase in his store after seeing the ad, and the average amount of those purchases. It's hardly an exact science.

Telesales organizations and catalogers have long tracked what advertisement customers are responding to by asking them, "Where did you hear about us?" or asking for a customer identification number from the back of a catalog. But the problem with this method is the same one that Bob has—many customers don't remember or care. Since they're the ones supplying the information, it will often be flawed, because customers forget where they learned about the company. Customers ordering using someone else's catalog, or ordering without a catalog, further skew the information.

But on the Web, customers are tracked accurately without even knowing it. As a company with a Web site, you can find out how many people visit your site, where they come from (another Web site that linked them to your site? a search engine?), how long they stay, what sections they browse, and for how long. If you ask visitors to the site to fill out a simple registration form, you can also tell who's a new visitor to the site and who's a repeat visitor. Plus, you can gather the type of demographic information that Carl Marbach of Avweb talks about in chapter 6—who your site's visitors are and what they are interested in.

This information is essential for companies that want to sell space on their Web site to advertisers. Advertisers want to know how long visitors stay during each visit, if the same visitors are returning again and again, what sections they're looking at and for how long, and what type of access they have (through a corporate account, government organization, or university). Advertisers pay for Web advertising using the same model as companies that pay for magazine or newspaper ads—prices are based on how many people read the publication. Web site tracking software can gather much more detailed information about readers than any newspaper or magazine can offer. Print publications can only give the number of subscribers and newsstand sales, not the number of actual readers each month. With Web tracking software, every company with a site can track how many people look at it each day.

Hit Rates

There are basically two ways of tracking visitors using software. The first dates back to the early days of the Web: A typical person visiting a Web site clicks on a page, enlarges a graphic, listens to a Web audio recording, leaves, and then comes back and makes other moves within the site. Each of those activities makes a request of the Web site host computer to send the visitor's computer some electronic information. Those requests are tracked as "hits." Basically, a hit registers each time a visitor clicks on part of the site. A hit also registers for each graphic or link on a page.

So if a visitor merely looks at a page with four graphics on it, that visitor registers as four hits. And if a visitor arrives at a particular site, then clicks on four different pages, plays a short video clip, gets disconnected, and comes back and clicks on two more pages before leaving, that particular visit registers as at least ten hits to the server software. So a site that claims 10,000 hits a week may in reality only have 2,000 visitors a week, each one clicking around the site five times before leaving. Or it could have 8,000 visitors a week, but most look only at the site's first page before leaving. Companies and ISPs have calculations for estimating how many visitors their hit rates translate to, but nobody knows for sure.

If the information is this unreliable, why are companies still using it? One reason is that the capability to track hit rates is already programmed into server software, so Web site developers don't have to buy extra software. Free software is also available on the Web for companies that want a separate software package offering a bit more detail than some server software. Rather than buy a complex software package or pay an ISP to track the information, companies using hit rates can simply rely on their server software or download the free software to get a general idea of the site's traffic and trend information.

This data is saved in files, which can then be reviewed on screen or printed out. If a Web site's server computer has a monitor attached to it, someone sitting at that computer can watch the hit rate information being gathered: If three people are looking at the site, the monitor would show the columns of data that track the visitors' progress through the pages. That information can be collected into a report as often as the company wants—daily, weekly, or most common, monthly. Some tracking reports are stored in a form compatible with database software, so they can be analyzed more easily. Companies can set up these hit rate data files to show whatever information in whichever order they choose.

Some ISPs and companies have adapted hit-rate tracking software to offer even more detailed information. In addition to hit rates, they can determine what browser software visitors are using, what site the user just came from (so a company can judge how many visitors come from a link from another site), what speed of modem the visitors are using (so the company can put fewer graphics on the site if most visitors are using very slow modems, for example), and what type of Internet access account the visitor has (commercial access or from a university or government organization). The software will also track error messages. For example, if the computer is overloaded when a visitor tries to play a video clip, and the visitor gets an error message saying that the clip is currently unavailable, the company sees that message on the hit rate log. So the company will know if there's a peak time when lots of error messages go out and can look for problems with the site's capability. Even with this additional data, a company that talks about visitors in terms of hit rates is still working with very vague information.

CASE STUDY

Select Comfort: Starting Out with Hit Rates

Select Comfort wanted to test a Web site before investing a lot of money in online development. The Minneapolis–based mattress retailer figured that simple hit rate information would be sufficient data to gauge the site's initial success after debuting it in mid 1995. Leslie Quigley, the company's manager of public relations, says, "We didn't even ask the developer if they could give us better tracking information."

"When the developer first explained what hit rates were, I realized that we wouldn't even consider relying on that little information in print advertising or TV," she says. "There are certainly a lot looser standards on the Web." But that's understandable, she figured, since it's a new medium: "It's not going to be perfect when you start out." The most helpful information she used was trending information, which told her if traffic was increasing or decreasing, and simple volume, which gave her a rough idea of how many people logged in. After a few months, company managers started asking for more detailed tracking information. But without a directive to invest more in an online strategy, Quigley didn't research tracking software or service options.

A year after going live with the site, the $30 million company concluded that enough people were visiting the site to make it worth expanding. Now Quigley is ready to step up to more-detailed and reliable tracking reports. "We'd like to know more closely who the visitors are and why they are there," she says. "Hit rate reports are sort of reliable but sort of not. You're not sure why somebody was at the site—whether they just searched for 'sleep' and got us but wanted something on sleep disorders. We want to be able to determine things like that."

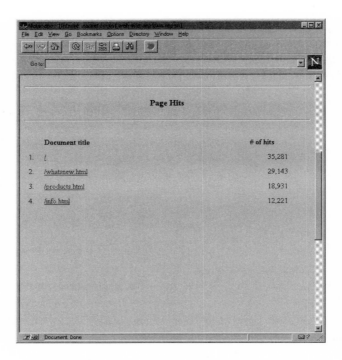

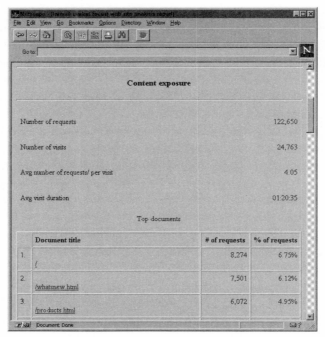

Hit rate printouts provide basic information on how many times a site is accessed. Tracking reports can be configured to provide more detailed visitor information.

Counting Visitors

A far more reliable tracking method is finding out how many actual visitors look at the site. Instead of tracking how many requests are made of the site's computer, this type of software works in one of two ways. One is really a glorified version of hit rates. A simple industry guideline is that ten hits equals one visitor, so hit rates are just divided by ten to provide "visitor" tracking. A more detailed approach involves applying a complex algorithm to a site's hit rates to calculate the number of actual visitors. But the most accurate method is by latching onto a visitor's home computer address at the moment the visitor arrives at the site and following that visitor until he or she leaves. This type of tracking reports where each visitor is and what he or she does. Sometimes visitors can tell they're being tracked by this method because the URL at the top of their screen has a string of characters at the end. When the Web user changes from screen to screen at the site, that string of characters—sometimes called a "cookie"—remains the same. Companies that want to use one of these tracking methods must buy a software package or pay a tracking service, which can come from the ISP where the site is stored or from a third-party auditing service.

Reports work pretty much the same as with hit rate software. When the system administrator (either at the ISP or the company itself) requests it, the tracking software processes a report of the traffic during a specific time period. In addition to providing traditional hit rate information, tracking reports offer some other categories: Where did visitors spend the most time within the site? How many visits did it take each user to reach the order page? Which advertisements elsewhere on the Web attracted the most visitors? What percentage are repeat visitors, and what percentage are new? How many repeat visitors originally found the site through an advertisement on the Web last month? These reports can then be imported into database programs like Microsoft Access or Excel for further massaging.

Available software packages will monitor a Web site no matter where that site is stored. Perhaps a company outsources its site to a service provider that doesn't provide suitable tracking reports. That company can generate its own by installing the software on the computer that hosts the Web site. (See the appendix for product information and price.)

Companies that outsource a site might decide to have the ISP handle the tracking reports. Many ISPs have the capability to offer only hit rate information, but some can provide more specific tracking reports, and a company that wants that valuable information may decide to choose a capable ISP several states away to get it. When choosing an ISP that offers tracking report services, ask how often they can provide regular reports. Also ask who will be available to help interpret and organize the data if someone at the company has a question. Then get a sample tracking report to make sure the information your company needs is covered and can be organized the way you want it. The ISP will most likely either run a fictional report or provide a real one with the company's name removed. That's because any company that signs a contract with an ISP for tracking reports should specify that the tracking information will be proprietary and won't be shown to prospective customers or media.

Auditors

Independent tracking services, such as Web Track or I/Pro, were formed to act as Web auditors by confirming or denying traffic reports claimed by companies. For example, if Sporty's Socks pays White Mountain Ski's site $800 per month for a pointer to their site, Sporty wants to make sure that White Mountain actually gets the number of visitors that they claim. If White Mountain claims to get 10,000 hits per month but only gets 6,000, Sporty is likely to get fewer visitors from White Mountain than expected. Therefore, the monthly pointer rates should be lower. Sporty might contract with an independent auditing service to make sure White Mountain actually gets 10,000 hits per month, or the service can just track the number of visitors coming from White Mountain. With this information, perhaps Sporty can strike a deal to pay White Mountain a sliding monthly fee based on the actual number of visitors who use the pointer. Sporty might also have the auditing service check the total traffic flow to his own site from anywhere else on the Web, to measure it against what his ISP reports each month.

CASE STUDY

Windham Hill Records: Tracking Visitors

Windham Hill Records, in Menlo Park, California, is one company that watches Web site traffic closely. Within three months of opening in late 1994, the $30 million record company's site quickly logged 300,000 visitors. That has settled

Windham Hill not only tracks visitors' progress through the site, but also asks visitors to register.

down to about 1,000 per day. Because Windham Hill relies on proprietary software created by its ISP, Interse, the company knows that those are 1,000 people, not just hits. When Windham Hill started looking around for Web developers where they could outsource the site, Roy Gattinella, vice president of marketing and new business development, knew enough to ask specifically about what type of tracking reports were available. Since he planned to use the information as a guideline for promoting particular artists, he wanted it to be as reliable as possible. Interse had developed proprietary software to track individual Web site visitors based on a combination of algorithm application and cookie tracking.

Gattinella gets reports from Interse every month. He decides how the information should be organized. The main information Gattinella looks for on the reports is summary and overview of how many visitors there were, the average time each spent at the site, and what sections they visited and for what length of time, which he calls the "click stream."

Based on that click stream feedback, Windham Hill has redesigned the site twice since its debut in late 1994. "We changed the whole navigation based on where people were going," Gattinella says. "Because we could analyze the click stream of individual visitors, we could direct traffic into parts of the site where we wanted people to go, like the bulletin board section. We saw that only fourteen percent of visitors made it to that area, so we added more links to get there from other pages. Now thirty-one percent go there."

Although the company wants the Web site reports to be as accurate and informational as possible, Windham Hill made a conscious decision not to insist that visitors register in order to be able to access the site. The company felt that visitors wouldn't want to be reminded that they were being overtly tracked.

Registering Visitors

With either type of traffic tracking, the names and email addresses of the visitors themselves usually remain anonymous unless they voluntarily provide it. If visitors provide that, they might also be willing to provide demographic information about themselves, such as where they live, their income level, and a few details about the family purchasing decisions. Gathering this data at Web sites is becoming more common as the Web grows. Companies need this information because it helps them focus the site to visitors' demographic profiles. Email addresses are important because mailing lists are valuable as a way to attract repeat visitors and recruit new ones by word of mouth.

Some companies require visitors to register before they can even access the site. (For more on the rationale behind requiring visitors to register, see the case study involving Avweb in chapter 6.) Basically, it works like this: Visitors to the site are able to see an introductory page, showing what information and entertainment the site offers. On that page, a notice explains that in order for advertisers to continue to sponsor the site, or in order for the company to customize the site to visitors upon their return, registration is necessary before the visitor can delve further. At that point, visitors can either leave or continue with the registration process. The registration form is usually only a page or two and usually doesn't ask for full names and mailing addresses. Most Web users don't want to provide that much personal information. Instead, surveys ask for general demographic information like age, interests, income, and family statistics. Once the form is filled out, visitors get a password to access the site.

The first company to require visitors to register was *Wired* magazine at their Web site, HotWired, in 1994. Visitors who registered were issued passwords in order to access the site. To return, visitors had to remember those passwords in order to gain entry to the site. HotWired was able to gather tracking information on repeat visitors—what they browsed at the site and how often they returned. The magazine used that data to become one of the first Web sites to sell advertising, making thousands of dollars per month from advertisers like Audi and setting a Web money-making precedent.

The biggest risk to registering visitors is that they may decide to just skip the site altogether rather than fill out the form. Many Web users dislike being tracked and will boycott sites that try. It's also very easy for visitors to throw off the statistics, and they gleefully do just that. At sites that require registration in exchange for a password, visitors lie about their demographic information. Knowing that they're being tracked, they click on information they don't really want. And once they leave, they give their password to others. For some time, HotWired's most popular visitor was "cypherpunk," a name linked to a password passed among countless users. That name topped HotWired's hit list month after month. Another risk to requiring visitors to register is that the data isn't completely accurate. Since visitors are volunteering the information, they're likely to just make something up when faced with a question like, "How many times in the past year have you bought shaving cream?" To get the most accurate results, keep the form simple and short.

CASE STUDY

Busey Bank: Encouraging Visitors to Register

"We've realized that the Web is not just an advertising medium but really an interactive medium," says Lisa Courtney, president of Busey Bank's online department. "People using it want to communicate, to put something in and get something back." By offering visitors a game as an incentive to register at the site, Courtney kills two birds with one stone. Not only do the visitors get a chance to interact and play, but the bank gathers demographic data on who comes to the site.

The $8 million bank in Champaign, Illinois, opened a Web site in mid 1994. In early 1995, the bank formed a separate department for online strategy. "Initially we viewed the Web as something very separate from banking," Courtney says. "Now it's becoming more involved in our overall marketing strategy." To check how effective the Web marketing is, the bank uses a software package called Illustra to track how customers move from page to page through the site and what path they take through the site before signing up for one of the bank's services.

To make that tracking information more meaningful, Busey wants to also gather basic demographic data from visitors in a short registration form. But unlike many other Web sites, Busey doesn't demand that all visitors register before they can access the site. Instead, the bank hopes to encourage visitors to register by offering useful information in return. "We don't want to make coming to the site very restrictive," Courtney says. "Hopefully, we offer something of value so they'll want to register." And since registration isn't mandatory, Courtney hopes that visitors will be less likely to be misleading on their responses.

How to Use the Data

It's not difficult to imagine how useful this tracking information can be. Imagine placing an ad in a wide-circulation magazine or newspaper. Imagine that every time somebody looks at that ad, a database tracks what they do. It tracks what the person looked at right before the ad, which tells whether or not the placement of the ad is successful. It tracks how long they looked at the ad, and what parts of the ad they read, which tells how compelling the ad is. And it tracks what the person does immediately after looking at the ad, whether or not they take action based on it. This kind of information can help drive a company's marketing decisions and product research. Gathering visitor feedback via email supplements this information. Companies have even set up virtual round-tables with customers online, to discuss future products or services or gather feedback on existing ones.

Tracking information can also work for a site immediately, before the company even sees the printouts. That information can be automatically tied to advertising at the site, whether those ads are for the site's products and services or for sponsors. Here's how the process works: A visitor to a real estate company's site fills out an online form asking for information about vacation property on the North Carolina coast. After clicking on the form and receiving in return a list of brokers in that area or properties for sale, the visitor might also see an ad for a mortgage company that specializes in vacation property financing, or an ad for a vacation time-share association. If the visitor clicks on those links for more information, the real estate company can track that process and show the mortgage company just how many visitors are being sent to them. That's one way to establish the value of those ads.

Not only is Web site tracking information useful, but it's essential for companies that want to make money on the Web. Companies need this tracking information to sell ads to other companies or sell links from their sites to others. Now that we've covered the options for gathering and organizing this information, let's look at the different ways that companies make money from their Web sites and how tracking data can help.

9

●●●●●●●●●●●●●●●●●●●●●●●●●●

Making Money:
Online Sales and Deals

People at companies interested in opening up a Web site usually have two burning questions: "What is the Web, exactly?" and "How do we make money online?" The previous chapters have explained what the Web is, how it works, and how to build and maintain a successful site—they've tackled the first question. Now let's get down to the business of making money. Not all Web sites will make money, and not all are supposed to. Some save the company money on expenses instead. Some are strictly promotional sites with payoffs that are hard to pin to exact dollar amounts. But any Web site, if properly maintained and monitored, can increase a company's visibility and usually it's profitability.

The most obvious way a Web site can boost profits is to increase sales without proportionately increasing labor or marketing expenses (see chapter 6 for a case study of how retailer Hot Hot Hot makes online sales). But companies interested in selling products or services on the Web should bear in mind that many customers are terrified of sending credit card numbers via email. The chances of someone stealing those credit card numbers is actually fairly remote—it's more likely that someone would steal the carbon copy of the customer's credit slip from a retail store's trash. The data that flows over the Internet's phone lines is available for hackers to steal, just as a store's garbage is fairly accessible to thieves. But it takes a lot of effort and expertise to take credit cards out of email messages or off a company's Web site computer. To assuage customer doubts and remove most of the risk, many companies offer some form of protected, safe transactions, either in the form of a software product or a transaction service.

In this chapter, the term "transactions" doesn't refer solely to sales. Any company that wants its Web site to be able to exchange information with visitors performs transactions. For example, a Web site might have a registration form that visitors fill out and return to the company. When the visitor clicks on the button that sends the form back, it's sent via email. That form can be stopped and copied anywhere along the way just as easily as a credit card number can. Although forms like that probably are not as valuable as a credit card number, some companies want to be able to reassure their Web site visitors that the information is protected.

Secret Codes

The software that protects transactions like this works just like the secret-message codes that soldiers used during World War I and II. Basically, a character or string of characters is substituted for each character in the original message. A simple example is that an "e" is always "7*" after it has been coded. The process of coding the message is called "encryption." For an encrypted message to make sense, the person—or in this case, software—receiving it must have the same code "key" as the sender, so that both sides realize that "7*" is supposed to mean "e."

The encryption process happens between the user's computer and the site computer. When a Web user is looking at a transaction form on a site, that form has been sent to the user's computer so the browser software can see it. The visitor to the Web site fills out the form, then clicks on a button that sends it back to the company. Immediately, the form's content is encrypted at the Web user's computer by the encryption software, then it's sent to the Web site computer over Internet phone lines. Once the message arrives, it's deciphered by the receiver's software, using the same key that the sender software used to program it. If it's intercepted along the way, it won't make any sense unless the person intercepting it also has the key that the sender and receiver have. The likelihood of that is fairly small, especially if the keys themselves haven't been sent over the Internet and possibly intercepted.

Versions of encryption software are available free on the Internet, including one of the best. Pretty Good Privacy (PGP) is widely acknowledged to be the most secure encryption software around. It's so good that its inventor, Phil Zimmerman, was recently under investigation for making it available worldwide. Encryption technology is considered to be a munition by the U.S. government, and by letting people in foreign countries download it, Zimmerman was accused of exporting munitions out of the United States. The investigation was eventually dropped. A commercial version of PGP is available from ViaCrypt (see appendix for information).

PGP protects against the possibility of the code key being stolen and used to decrypt intercepted messages by creating a private key and a public key. The company using the software keeps the private key and uses the public key to encrypt all messages at the other end. Only the private key decrypts the messages. Not even users with copies of the public key can decrypt messages that have been coded with it. Anyone using ViaCrypt's software can also create encrypted email messages to send to the company: Request a copy of the company's public key (available at the Web site or by calling or emailing the company) and put that into the software, then hit the "encrypt" button when sending email.

This software is used mostly to authenticate the identity of the person sending the email message. A company using PGP might give the public key to all telecommuting employees, for example, so that the email they send is verifiably from them and not from some prankster or hacker. But some small companies also use it at their Web sites, for customers placing orders and sending credit card numbers in email messages. By using this software, the company can assure customers that their email is encrypted and protected. (Encryption software packages are available from other manufacturers as well; see appendix for details.)

Netscape's Web browser dominates the market, with more than 75 percent of the people who use the Web viewing it through Netscape Navigator. Because of its popularity, many companies that put up Web sites use Netscape's Secure Commerce Web server software. The latest version of that software also contains encryption capability (as does Enhanced Mosaic). The browser software encrypts anything that a visitor to the Web site (using Netscape's browser) emails back to the computer that stores the site, so the visitor can safely place an order by sending a credit card number over the Internet, either in an email message or listed on an order form. The problem with Netscape's encryption software is that it only works between a Netscape browser and a Netscape-served Web site; the Commerce Server package costs about $5,000.

One problem with encryption software is that some Web users can't take advantage of it. If they're using another Web browser, Netscape encryption might not work, or perhaps they're accessing the Web from work, where there's a firewall. Sometimes those firewalls don't allow encrypted messages to pass through to the Internet. To offer secure sales and other transactions without handling encryption, a company can contract with a transaction service.

Transaction Services

The transaction services area of the Web is undergoing many changes, with new systems popping up almost every day. Just as consumers today can shop with a check, cash, or various credit cards, Web consumers of tomorrow will continue to have many purchasing options. Merchants shouldn't assume that any one online transaction service or software will dominate the market anytime soon.

Different types of services are available as well. One type does what a company using encryption software would do, basically processing customer credit card sales by encrypting them for each customer. Another type offers a form of digital cash transactions that go through an approved bank. Yet another type handles transactions entirely over the phone, never sending any information over the Internet. The disadvantage to all of these is that consumers can't make purchases as immediately as if they just sent a credit card number. Following are outlines of three of the transaction services geared toward smaller companies, with a brief description of how each works and what it costs to use.

CyberCash

CyberCash transactions move among three separate software programs. One must be loaded onto the company's Web site computers. The second, called a "wallet," must be loaded onto the consumer's computer. The third program is on the CyberCash computers. The merchant and consumer software is free.

If Bill wants to buy a bottle of wine from Virtual Vineyards' Web site, he would select a bottle and fill out the wine retailer's online order form, complete with shipping information. Virtual Vineyards then emails an invoice to Bill requesting payment. Bill can launch the CyberCash wallet if he already has it, or he can go get it if he doesn't. Depending on which option Bill chooses, he can pay in a matter of minutes. Once Bill has the CyberCash wallet and wants

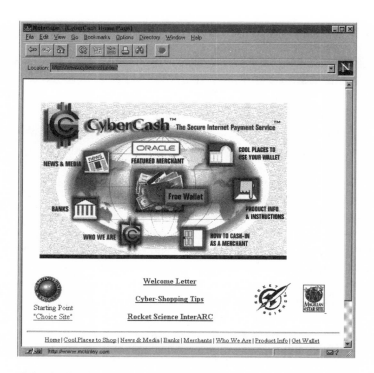

CyberCash offers the capability for merchants to sign up for transaction service at their Web site.

to order again at Virtual Vineyards, he simply clicks on their "pay" button. Then the CyberCash software on the wine company's computer sends a special message to Bill's computer, which prompts the CyberCash wallet to open on his computer. Bill chooses which credit card he wants to use and clicks on it. All of these email messages are automatically encrypted as they whiz among the three parties on the Internet and the conventional credit card networks that are connected directly to the CyberCash servers. The merchant is paid as if the sale were a normal credit card transaction, CyberCash makes money from the banks that handle each sale.

DigiCash

Cheaper for merchants to use than some other services, DigiCash appeals to those who are selling low-margin items. Say Sarah wants to buy a pair of shoes from Heel-to-Toe's Web site. She loads DigiCash's software onto her computer, then uses that to send money—using a credit card or ATM card—to an

DigiCash is a popular transaction service with small businesses.

approved bank, using an encrypted email message. The bank sends back an encrypted email message with a list of numbers. That string of numbers represents the amount of money the consumer sent. Then Sarah returns to Heel-to-Toe's site and emails them her string of numbers. Heel-to-Toe forwards those numbers to the issuing bank, which deposits the money in the shoe company's account. The bank tracks all issued numbers that are used in case any are lost, so it can replace them. In mid 1996, DigiCash was still testing this service, signing up merchants for free trials.

First Virtual Holdings

This service claims it is the safest of all because consumers never send their credit numbers over the Internet. Say Lisa wants to buy an online book from Bibliobytes' Web site. She clicks on the First Virtual button at the bookstore's site and signs up for the service, giving First Virtual her name, email address, and a personal identification number, or PIN, that she creates. FV then emails

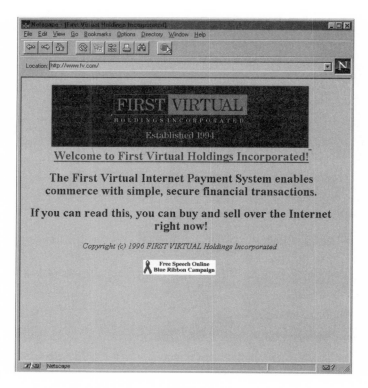

First Virtual is experimenting with a form of electronic cash for secure transactions.

Lisa a toll-free number to call with her credit card number, which they put on file and also bill for a $2 sign-up fee. Then First Virtual emails Lisa and tells her that her account is ready to go. Lisa goes back to Bibliobytes and enters her PIN to authorize the sale. First Virtual receives the transaction information and matches the PIN to Lisa's credit card number, which is on file, then sends her an email asking her to confirm that she made the purchase. If so, First Virtual processes the transaction with the bank and makes a deposit into the merchant's account after subtracting twenty-nine cents per sale and 2 percent of the sale price. Merchants sign up by paying First Virtual $10 and supplying a checking account number and other information.

First Virtual service has traditionally been used only to sell information, like software, over the Internet. The company is rolling out a new model for product merchants that includes the extra step of emailing the merchant once the consumer's credit card has been authorized to trigger product shipment. Merchants approved by First Virtual's bank get paid in a few days but must pay about $250 to sign up. Nonapproved merchants can sign up for the $10 fee but don't receive their payment for ninety days.

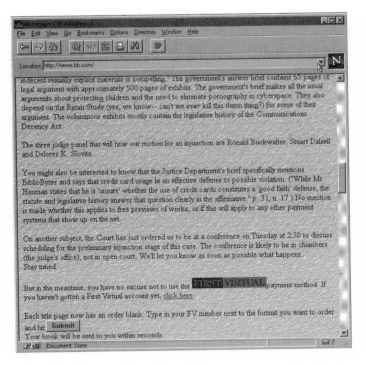

Bibliobytes bookstore offers First Virtual in addition to other transaction methods.

Other Sales Options

Using encryption software or a transaction service isn't the only way that companies can process online sales. Some ISPs will handle transactions for their clients. Many have already contracted with one of the transaction services and so can offer secure transactions as part of their Web site service. Another way that ISPs process transactions is to gather email orders from sites and then fax those directly to a company or its warehouse. The email orders sent to the ISP might or might not be encrypted. (For more information on this method, see the case study of the Hot Hot Hot site in chapter 6.)

Some companies prefer to handle transactions themselves, either to save the money that would be paid out for software or to a service or simply to have more direct control over the process. The easiest method of doing online sales is to receive customers' unencrypted credit card numbers. Industry experts agree that this procedure is reasonably safe for online shoppers, at least as safe as giving a credit card number over the telephone or in a retail store. It's much more difficult to intercept an email order and pull out the credit card number than it is for a retail or telephone salesperson to simply write it down. And many customers seem to agree. By the end of 1995, more than 2.5 million consumers had already made purchases on the Web. Many consumers, however, do have the perception that it's dangerous. Whether or not that's true doesn't matter—if consumers think it is, they won't buy this way. Although it may be only a few customers who won't risk unencrypted transactions at your company's Web site, why lose any of those sales?

CASE STUDY

Virtual Vineyards: Offering Consumers Many Ways to Buy

"My goal is to get paid," says Robert Olson of Virtual Vineyards. "It's not my goal to invent new technology." The online wine retailer opened an in-house Web site in January 1994 and offers several different ways for customers to make online purchases. Virtual Vineyards takes mailed checks, faxed orders, emailed credit card orders, encrypted credit card orders, and pur-

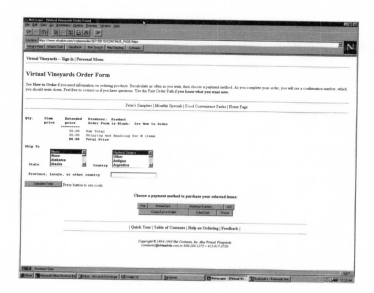

The only form of payment that Virtual Vineyards doesn't accept is cash.

chases made via the CyberCash transaction service. "The only thing we wouldn't know what to do with is cash," says Olson.

The encryption software is included in Olson's Netscape Commerce Server software. Most of his customers use a Netscape browser to view the site. When those customers send any email to Virtual Vineyards—whether it has a credit card number in it or not—that email is automatically encrypted by the browser software, and then unencrypted after it arrives at Olson's server software. Because the feature is included, Olson didn't have to pay extra to offer encryption as an option for customers using Netscape.

The CyberCash option is free to merchants. CyberCash makes its money from the banks that process the transactions and by charging a small fee to consumers when they make a transaction. In mid 1996, only about 5 percent of Virtual Vineyards' sales were to customers using CyberCash.

Although he offers these options, Olson says 75 percent of his orders come via regular email, and about 35 percent of all online orders arrive in email with an unencrypted credit card. Because of this, Olson doesn't store any of those credit cards on his Internet computer, even though he has a firewall. "The public relations disaster would be if someone stole our credit cards," he says. "Twenty thousand credit cards sitting in one file that someone could suck up—a lot of merchants don't understand that this is where the risk is.

"There's no standard for online sales right now," Olson says. "And it's not clear why any merchant should care. They should be independent of loyalty toward one type of transaction option." Olson compares online transactions to traditional retail transactions, for which most consumers have a walletful of credit cards from which to choose. Why be a store that limits customers to only one of those payment methods?

Rather than risk alienating customers who want the assurance of secure transactions, some companies don't perform online sales at all. Instead, they list a toll-free phone number and address for customers who wish to place an order. The big disadvantage is that this option won't collect the impulse buys that other methods will. The main reason is that most consumers browsing the Web from home only have a single phone line into the house. If they're logged on to the Web on that phone line, they can't pick up the phone or send a fax at the same time. They have to wait to log off before they can call or send a fax to buy the item. By that time, it's highly likely that they've either forgotten about it or they're too tired or busy to follow through.

Global Sales

That first overseas order is one of the biggest suprises for many small companies with Web sites that sell a product or service. Most countries in the world have Internet access, and consumers in those countries can visit the Web just as easily as we do in the U.S. In fact, for many overseas Internet users, the Web is the only place that they can purchase certain products and services that aren't available in their country. Your company's site could become quite popular overseas, so it's best to acknowledge that possibility early and address it in the online strategy and on the site itself.

First, decide whether or not your company is ready to ship product overseas, or if the service for sale can be performed for overseas customers. This might not be an issue for companies that already have international customers, unless there are countries the company doesn't do business with for one reason or another. Prepare for the fact that orders could come from any country, and think about what to charge for shipping. Study up on legal issues to be aware of in other countries. Canada, for example, has certain laws governing how free prizes are distributed in promotional contests. Other countries have strict laws about what can and can't be sold there.

Some companies decide that they prefer not to process overseas sales rather than work through these issues. Others want the additional revenue and are ready to debut the Web site but have yet to figure out how they'll charge for shipping or handle foreign currency. The easiest solution to both problems is to design a message on the site itself that says something like, "Sales made in U.S. dollars and shipped to U.S. addresses only." Another option for companies interested in overseas sales is to post a message on the order form asking overseas customers to call the company for preferred purchase currency and shipping information. Obviously, this only works when international sales volume is low. Otherwise it would be very time-consuming to calculate shipping charges for each sale. But it is a good way to gauge international response to the site before establishing general pricing guidelines. Some companies charge a flat fee for shipping overseas; others charge what it actually costs, depending on destination and package weight.

Whether or not your company is ready to handle overseas sales, it is still a good idea to make sure the site is one that overseas visitors can understand. The main thing to bear in mind, of course, is that not all visitors to the site will understand English well. That shouldn't be a problem—the Web, with its colorful graphics, is a terrific medium for communicating across language barriers. Simple illustrations of what the different sections of the site offer will help make navigating easier for non–native English speakers or for any visitor. For example, small illustrations or photos of products with prices next to them would make the point fairly clearly that something is for sale. Choosing a few graphic elements that repeat from page to page shows visitors that they're staying within the same site. A small graphic of a musical note can be linked with an audio clip and a movie reel linked with a video clip. Try to keep graphics simple and universal. Just make sure that the site doesn't become so graphics-heavy that it takes forever to download.

CASE STUDY

EquiSearch: Surprised by International Sales

Andy Griscom was surprised when he received his first international sale at EquiSearch's Web site. Although he knew the books for sale at his equine products and services site would probably attract international buyers, he hadn't thought about how to charge for shipping. The $2 charge over and above the book price wouldn't cover shipping from his Westerly, Rhode Island, location to the British customer.

"I sent the book anyway," he says. The customer used an American Express credit card number, to which Griscom billed an extra $2 for shipping and let the credit card company handle the currency conversion. But then Griscom formulated a plan. He calculated an average weight for his books by weighing twenty random books together, then dividing that number by twenty. Then he researched how much it would cost to ship that weight to each overseas country. "Some countries are $1.50 and some are $6.50," he learned. "I have to pass that along." To avoid currency issues, he takes payment only in U.S. dollars.

Complicating matters, Griscom had to decide which overseas shipper to use. "You can pick FedEx, UPS, or the postal service—whichever is cheapest depends on the country," he says. "I don't have time to do that for each country, so I'm going with the postal service no matter what. If I lose a little, I lose a little." He admits he could also save money by drop-shipping books directly from the publishers, but instead he warehouses them himself. "I want to write a personal letter to include in the front cover of every book that thanks the customer and includes my card," he says. "We want to keep it a little 'down-home on the farm' to counteract the high-tech side of things."

Other Ways to Make Money

So far we've talked about the different ways to sell to Web users. But there are ways that companies can make money from their Web sites without even processing online transactions. One way that companies are beginning to experiment with is to charge Web users for visiting the site. Because there are so many other interesting sites online, charging to access your site can be risky. Web users might just skip it and go somewhere else. So this model only works if companies have specific, useful information that users want. Some charge customers to search through and download specific information from part of a Web site. That's about all customers are willing to pay for right now. A more reliable model is to have other companies pay for the Web site somehow, like charging for pointers from your company's site to theirs.

CASE STUDY

electronic **Gourmet Guide:** *Selling Links*

"We get zillions of people emailing us and asking for links," says Kate Heyhoe, editor of the Web's electronic *Gourmet Guide* site, an electronic magazine about gourmet cooking. Heyhoe says, "Our policy now is that we don't automatically do mutual links." (Mutual links go from eGG to another site, and from the other site back to eGG.) Many Web site administrators just go ahead and trade those links with compatible sites, without charging for them. eGG, however, makes money on those deals. "Web site linking is valuable," Hayhoe says. "And we bring more to a lot of sites than others out there, so we don't pay. We expect people to pay us."

When another site administrator—say, from a cooking utensil catalog—calls Heyhoe to ask if eGG is interested in linking to the catalog, the first thing she considers is the site's value. How many users regularly visit the catalog? Is it a broader audience than eGG draws on its own? Is it the target audience that eGG strives to reach? This type of information is available from a Web site's tracking or hit rate reports. Second, Heyhoe looks at the quality of the other site. Is it easy for users to get home— back to eGG—again, or will eGG just be sending them out into limbo land? Does the site take too long to load onto the computer? "We've branded eGG and want to keep the image as a responsible site with top quality," Heyhoe says.

If the answers fit eGG's profile, they'll strike a deal with the other site, charging a monthly fee. Many Web sites just trade mutual links without charging a fee. Those that do charge anywhere from a few hundred dollars a month to a few thousand. "The financial structure of the Web changes every day," Heyhoe says, "so the rate cards that existed last month have already changed. It's a free-for-all, and the value a site can establish depends on the individual advertiser. Is the value in getting people to the site? Or is it in getting products off the shelf?"

Another creative way to make money without making actual sales is to charge advertisers. Those advertisers might pay for a billboard type ad, or they might buy classified ads on your company's site. In order to command respectable rates for this, your company has to convince the advertiser of your site's value. It can do that by demonstrating impressive hit rates, tracking reports or by showing the advertiser what leads your site generates.

CASE STUDY

Aircraft Shopper Online: Selling Classified Ads

"We're convinced that this is the way that large-ticket items like aircraft will be sold," says Tony Friend of Aircraft Shopper

Online, a Web site with classified advertising for airplanes. Friend has been running ASO since mid 1995. "We think we've carved out a niche," he says. The site's goal is to be completely advertising-supported.

The way ASO makes money on the in-house site is by charging the aircraft owners or brokers who want to list their classified ad online. Ads for corporate airplanes cost $1.64 per day. Ads for smaller, private airplanes are 84 cents per day. That buys the small-plane advertiser room for a full specification sheet and up to three photographs of the aircraft. Corporate-plane sellers can send as many specs and photos as they like. Friend estimates that the sell cycle for aircraft is about four months. On any given day he has at least 850 classified ads on his site; 25 percent of those are corporate jets and turbo-prop aircraft and 75 percent are smaller private planes. Friend doesn't ask advertisers for a

Aircraft Shopper Online earns money at the site by charging for classified advertising like this.

percentage of the sale price because he doesn't want to compete with the aircraft brokers that place many of the ads on his site.

Friend's ISP sends him hit rate reports, but instead of relying on those to impress his advertisers and justify his rates, Friend gets even more specific. He shows advertisers how many leads he generates for them. "When we send the bills out, we can say, 'We sent you nine leads on that aircraft,' " he says. "Counting information like that is more important than unreliable hit rates." What he does use hit rate reports for is trend information. "We've seen a steady hit rate increase by about 30 percent every two months."

Although the site wasn't yet profitable by mid 1996, Friend expects it will be within the next few years. "Advertisers are just starting to see serious responses," he says. "People are telling them they saw the aircraft on the Internet." Friend is optimistic that consumer response will drive the attitude of advertisers, who will be more likely to invest in his Web site.

Once a company sets up a successful, busy, and profitable Web site, the next step is to think about the future. What's in store for the Web during the next few years? That time span can be a lifetime for a marketplace that's already grown from not much more than an idea to a bustling commercial center in two years. But industry experts and analysts hazard guesses in the next chapter. They predict what the next changes will be for the Web, and what small businesses can do now to prepare.

10

• •

Gazing into the Future:
Experts Tell What's Next

A medium that changes as rapidly as the Web is difficult to forecast. Without established models, how is a company to know what path to follow or what future to prepare for? That's part of the excitement for businesses on the Web. They're defining the new marketplace at the same time that they're growing their online presences. Although the arena is wide open and nobody can predict exact developments, industry analysts have opinions about which areas are likely to be "hot" over the next few years. Here are the thoughts of some of the Web's most knowledgeable experts, the people who are investing in new development, creating new products, and servicing this new industry. They offer insight and advice to companies anxious to prepare for what's next in Web development.

DAN LYNCH

In the 1980s, Dan Lynch founded Interop, a popular computer and interactive trade show that now focuses on the Internet. After selling that company to Ziff-Davis in 1990, Lynch started investing in Internet-related companies, including

CyberCash, UUNET Technologies, and InfoSeek. He thinks that small companies will have trouble establishing themselves in the Web's next paradigm, advertising-sponsored sites:

> *I see hard times. I see huge success for some companies, but also some sites overbuilding. The problem with the Web is it's either a level playing field or a killing field. Everyone can be there, and you can look just as big as IBM. But that's going to piss off IBM. They'll figure out a way to take this medium, which appears to be democratic, and tilt the playing fields back in their favor. Rather than just advertising on the Web, they'll have events that are interesting infotainment and will be "brought to you by . . . IBM." Small companies won't be able to spring for sponsorships like this. The little guys with little sites—think of them as specialty magazines with narrow audiences. The problem is that these little publications can't mount a sales force to visit potential advertisers.*
>
> *I think little guys are in deep trouble because they're not a big enough buy for advertisers. The person they're talking to at the ad agency needs to buy $100,000 worth of stuff, but the little site is only worth $5,000. Little sites selling products and service will be lost in the crowd. There will start to be aggregation services that look at all the stuff on Web and put that together with advertisers.*
>
> *To be attractive to advertisers, the little guy needs to be conducting readership research. Those sites will have to be able to describe their readership profile to advertisers. They'll have to find that out in a way that's valid and not intrusive. My advice to small businesses is to get that demographic information on one sheet of paper and spread it as far and wide as you can.*

BILL WASHBURN

The first executive director of the Commercial Internet Exchange, Bill Washburn has focused on bringing the Internet to the business community since early 1992. Coming from an academic background, Washburn realized early how significant the Internet could be to the commercial world. After leaving CIX in 1994, Washburn joined Mecklermedia, the large Internet publisher and trade-show organizer. As vice president for Internet business development, he works with companies to help them develop strategic visions for how to use the Internet in their companies. He is very excited about the Web's effect on global competition and information sharing:

> *One thing we'll see on Web in the next few years is the intro-duction of the mobility of culture. If you go around the globe, you notice that it's not that different anymore in so many ways, because so many things already have global distribution. In particular, American music and fashion come to mind. We've got to start recognizing that this mobility is going to put every-one on a similar field of play. We'll see people competing with us for jobs, for how we create new business, how we make exist-ing business function more efficiently. The Web puts everything at our fingertips. You don't have to be a well-financed business executive to have access. You can be in Malaysia or Milan, not just Manhattan, and still have access to the latest ideas and most innovative new uses of technology. That's what the Web is going to do.*
>
> *That's going to mean more competition, but that's not bad because there will be more and more niches. One thing that scares people is their underlying assumption that this is a zero-sum game. They think, "If I'm in competition with more people, there will be a thinning out of the wealth and I'll have less." But what happens instead is a greater increase in demand for prod-ucts and information.*
>
> *Think of it this way: 150 years ago Edison created the way to record sounds. At first, people who made a living giving con-certs decided to refuse to record. They thought that if they recorded their voices, nobody would ever want to pay to listen to them in concert. And what happened? Recording didn't reduce the demand for performances, it increased it. Recording became a form of advertisement, a way to increase value and visibility. Then radio came on the scene, and record companies thought it would destroy demand for recordings. What hap-pens? The opposite again, it creates more demand for records. There's a truth under this—the sharing of information makes it more valuable. It's a dynamic that we don't truly understand yet; it's about how information sharing creates demand.*

To get ready, companies need to start participating. The key to the Web is acting and interacting; you can't understand it in the abstract. Then, you will begin to have in your organization a massive flow of ideas about partnering and sharing with different people, even your competitors. Be prepared for that and allow it. The organizations that open themselves up to this and let control go, let everyone play with it, they will be the ones having fantastic new ideas. Small companies have an edge in that they're more open to partnerships and more willing to be fast moving. Their glory days are in front of them, and they know that. They know that the only game in town is to just go for it.

DAN NOVA

Dan Nova is a partner at @Ventures, a venture capital fund formed in early 1995. The fund is a division of CMG, a publisher of Web-related magazines and owner of the search engine Lycos. @Ventures is the only venture capital fund that focuses solely on Internet-related investments, finding companies in very early stages of development. In early 1996, it was halfway through its $40 million fund, had closed about nine deals, and was planning to go to market for another $75 to $100 million. Nova has very specific ideas about what types of companies will be successful on the Web in the coming years:

Nineteen ninety-five was the year of the browser; 1996 will be year of the search engines. Yahoo!, Lycos, InfoSeek will all go public. It will also be the year of agent technology, and personalization of information will be a lot more available to the end user. Say I search on the Web for information on merger activity, the Boston Celtics, and Chinese cooking. The advertiser doesn't know I'm Dan Nova, but it does have very unique information about me. You'll start to see more auto-insertion of ads at sites based on that information.

The other thing you'll see in 1996 and 1997 is intranet technologies. Corporations now can communicate with customers and employees on a lot more effective basis using internal Web sites. More and more companies will develop technology for the intranet sites, like the application of voice. Voice becomes just another data format, so every morning an employee can get a message from the CEO at the home page.

Nineteen ninety-seven and 1998 will be the years where content companies start to blossom. Successful sites will be those focusing on specific subject areas, like a golf site, finance site, or health care site. Those will cut deep vertical seams tying in both content and community, and they'll be advertiser sponsored. For example, wouldn't it be nice to know there's a comprehensive health care site with information and community? A Web user can look up breast cancer and find research, then also chat with other people about different treatments. It's that tying-in of community that really adds value to that content. There's instantaneous feedback and market research on products and services [that] consumers are looking to evaluate.

To compete online, I think it's very important to be early. First-move advantage is very important. Grabbing mind share and market share will continue to be critical. For example, Lycos's search engine has better technology than Yahoo!'s, but Yahoo! grabbed mind and market share very quickly, so it's continuing to do well. There's still a tremendous opportunity for entrepreneurs to enter into a marketplace as a first, second, or third player, develop good content, and compete with the larger players.

It's also important to realize that you can't apply traditional media rules; you have to be new, innovative, creative, and appeal to the Internet culture, which is very unique. If a big company can think like a small company, they'll do well. But big companies are often slow to react, bureaucratic, and they trip over themselves in making decisions. Small companies are willing to take risks. Think about links, thing about strategic relationships. Think outside the box.

BLANE ERWIN

Forrester Research is a consulting firm that regularly surveys the online community to scout industry trends and make forecasts. Talking to large and small businesses, analysts at Forrester generate statistics and provide overviews of what new models will emerge. Blane Erwin is an analyst at Forrester, and his study of the Web focuses on how it will change the order fulfillment process for small companies:

We're almost to the point where any small company that can afford an Internet connection and browser will be able to start prospecting, promoting, paying, and exchanging purchase orders and invoices electronically. With the Web, they'll have the interactivity and low cost of entry to get into Electronic Data Interchange (EDI). But a merchant won't want to handle the different steps of that process. There has to be some sort of software module that sits in between the Web pages that display products and the pages that handle the transaction software. Someone has to own that whole messy business of order fulfillment and things like order re-entry if some didn't go through. If handling orders includes shipping a product, a merchant isn't going to want to go to the Federal Express site and deal with tracking the packages.

Small companies will reach the point where they will have a simple Web storefront collecting information about what products or services customers want to buy. But once it's time to bundle the whole transaction, customers will be linked transparently to the third-party Web site that will put together the whole transaction—payment, preferred shipper, everything.

What's going to happen is that traditional EDI companies will move to the Web to offer this type of service. EDI vendors are obsessed with reaching small- to medium-size businesses. They've tapped out the big users. The holy grail that everyone is going after on the Web is to somehow touch the transactions, and that's where activity will be focused for the next while.

To prepare for this change, companies should find an Internet service provider now that can host, develop the site, and offer transaction services. There's a whole range of players going after this business. I'm guessing that the costs will probably be around $1,000 per month. If you're making the long-term decision to have customers be able to order from your site, we think that narrows the field of Web developers and ISPs down to someone with transaction capability.

ED KROLL

Ed Kroll is a member of the National Center for Supercomputing Applications at the University of Illinois at Champaign-Urbana, a center for Internet devel-

opment. In 1992, he wrote *The Whole Internet,* the definitive guide that introduced many readers to this new medium. His perspective is one of how the Web
will change for consumers:

> *First of all, the whole issue of security to me is sort of news-
> paper hysteria and not real. If you think about what happens in a
> restaurant, where you throw your credit card on a little plate and
> they make copies—the Internet is more secure than any restau-
> rant has ever been. Despite that, I think that secure Netscape will
> be deployed, and everyone will use it. By and large, it will soothe
> people's minds rather than do anything useful.*
>
> *Java design for the Web isn't going to be a big deal. Every-
> one's talking Java, but it executes slowly and downloads slowly. Is
> the consumer really going to care that much that your logo is ani-
> mated? The answer is no. It's going to go the way of big corporate
> logos that were popular when Web first came out. Everyone put
> their one-megabyte logo out there and it made people mad to wait
> for it to download. The same thing will happen with Java.*
>
> *Right now, searching the Web is sort of like going to the
> library and someone tells you the book you probably need is on
> the third floor, second row, first shelf, fourth from the end. Well,
> if that turns out not to be the book you need, you have no way of
> knowing that the one you really need is right next to it, on the
> second shelf instead. That's going to change. We will continue to
> have combinations of search engines, like Point Communica-
> tions and Yahoo! with their edited lists, and then search engines
> like Alta Vista or Lycos that scan the whole Web. Between the
> two types, people will have a reasonable shot at finding just
> about anything they want on the Web.*
>
> *What will change is that people will also be able to ask for
> things on the Web by name. For example, think about trying to
> get the president's State of the Union address. You may have an
> address for the site, but if that site is down or busy, you can't get
> it. But soon, instead of typing in that address you'll be able to
> type in "state of the union" and get automatically linked to a
> site that has it and is available. Companies will have multiple
> server computers for a Web site, and users will automatically
> get bounced between them based on which one has the lightest
> load. Things will move faster with less likelihood of mistakes.*

RONNIE PETERS

Ronnie Peters has been working in the forefront of Web design for several years. He has worked with large companies like IBM, Reader's Digest, and the Discovery Channel, and also with smaller businesses like EquiSearch. The founder of Infogram, a Web design firm based in New York, Peters thinks that the future of Web design will separate the "haves" from the "have nots":

> *Right now because of the bandwidth problem, the Web is a pretty level playing field. It doesn't matter if you're NBC or a plumbing store, you're under the same kind of constraints. But soon we'll see cable modem access and higher bandwidth capabilities. Then you'll see an incredible drifting apart of the companies that can afford entertainment-style design and those who can't.*
>
> *The initial rush and excitement to get on the Web will be taken over by the maturing of the market. Already you can see how rapidly it's changed. The first thing was for a company just to have a Web presence. Now it's important to have a* good *presence. Companies are starting to recognize how important it is to have a well-designed site.*
>
> *The Web is a very even playing field right now. If I do a search for jeans, I get the most simple fashion sites coming up alongside Levi's, one of the most sophisticated sites around. The listings are all side by side, with same-size type and billing. But soon, companies will start doing what happens in the yellow pages. Those with money can put larger listings on the Web, others will just have a single line of black type. I think that also, over the next few years, you'll see some people giving up on the Web. They've gone in and tried it and realized it's just not the way to promote their product, service, or company.*
>
> *Entertainment giants and corporations who can throw a lot of money at the Web will do dynamic elaborate programming. But that kind of thing will be prohibitively expensive, and small companies won't be able to have full-motion graphics and sound. To compete, they'll need to emphasize the quality of content. It's like TV, where you get those attorneys that have commercials that look like someone set up a video camera in the guy's office. They're very crude commercials, but there's a definite, clear message.*

Think of value-added content. You would think that Federal Express has a really mundane service, but they have an incredibly popular site because it offers really valuable information—people can track their packages. Even tiny companies have a really good chance if they can figure out what message they have that's useful.

MARC ANDREESSEN

While still a student at the University of Illinois at Champaign-Urbana, Marc Andreessen led the team that created Mosaic, the Web's first software browser capable of viewing graphics. He then went into partnership with Jim Clark, one of the founders of Silicon Graphics, to start Netscape Communications Corporation. The browser and Web server software he developed there quickly dominated the industry. Andreessen is in the forefront of Web product design, and he offers insight into what the Web will look like next:

One of the obvious things is that the Web is basically going to keep doubling every eight to ten months. The number of businesses online is going to grow faster. The problem with not getting engaged right now is that most businesses are pretty deep in experimentation mode, and the learning curve is getting longer because the Web is getting more sophisticated. My basic warning to businesses not yet engaged is that when they finally realize they have to, it might be too late because the curve will be too long. This stuff moves pretty fast.

The no-brainer reason for any small company to get online today is email. It's a customer connection that doesn't require any effort to establish. It doesn't matter what the business is, some large number of customers will have email addresses.

We're trying to make it easier for businesses to build communities around products and image. A community can pull customers together and give them support, get them to buy more and get others engaged. Video telephony over the Web is going to be a big thing. To prepare for this, a small business should start looking at value-added resellers, or VARs. A lot of the top VARs are into the whole Web thing; they can set up and link the Web into other systems in your company and do it in a personalized way.

Also it's important to hire someone to bring in-house who already knows how to do Web stuff. You want to be serving in-house over the long term for better control. You want to be able to change things whenever you need to. It's better because of scale—if your site gets really busy and you get a lot of traffic, your ISP can get overloaded and angry. And if you serve in-house, you can tie the site into order processing and link it to your back-end database. Much of what big companies are doing involves running a database internally for customer support—Federal Express is a great example. They took their system and built a gateway to it and put it on the Web. They save millions of dollars because they don't have to have people sitting on the phone.

Transactions are pretty straightforward at this point. There are some things that will sell really well, some that won't. If you can get the proper exposure, it can work. There are examples of successful bookstores, food delivery, music, software, but there's not a great example of someone selling toilet paper over the Web yet. The Web is basically a variation of real life. If you put a hot sauce shop in a 2,000-person town, you probably won't sell too much hot sauce. If you sell a few other things, offering variety with strong brand image and advertising and you're in a popular location with a lot of traffic, like New York, you'll do well.

Vin Cippola

Vin Cippola is a board member of the Electronic Frontier Foundation (EFF), a nonprofit civil liberties group started by Lotus founder Mitch Kapor and John Perry Barlow. EFF was founded to address and protect privacy, intellectual property, and transaction issues for companies and individual consumers using the Internet. Cippola thinks that small companies can be at risk when jumping on the Web bandwagon too quickly:

I think there's going to be profound change over the next couple of years. A lot of companies are rushing to use the Web even though it isn't producing the results that the hype has led them to believe. Small businesses with constrained resources can easily get into trouble. Many markets are not yet engaged with this technology enough for some small businesses to be investing their future in the technology. To succeed, the key thing is to observe how one's market continues to evolve, and assess at what point it becomes prudent to get involved with the Web. As a business, if you stay customer-focused and pay attention to what customers are telling you, and let that lead you, you'll be okay. When you try to anticipate customer interaction anecdotally, you get into trouble. Very often we've done bail-out programs for organizations that have applied abundant resources to the wrong channels way in front of what the market would bear.

Having said that, we all recognize that electronic communication is going to be an absolutely major gateway of commercial transaction. Many things that aren't in that venue now will increasingly be. Everybody needs to get on, there's no question. But it's different for small businesses. The time to get on is when you have some strength and aren't relying on this new technology to deliver customers.

Companies that are on the Web now should measure very closely what success they're having. They really have to adopt very flexible strategies. Part of the problem in the future will be whether or not contemporary models are sustainable. For example, are these the ways that companies will perform transactions six months from now? Nobody knows this yet. Models will be created that will be broken and won't be sustainable, so companies have to be flexible and not overinvest in today's models because they're going to change.

There isn't any packaged media approach for anyone. The Web will always be about customized solutions, and those are the best solutions. Right now there's a lot of replication with people copying one another. Copycat strategies are usually short-lived. A business should go through some strategic planning processes so it can really get at the soul of the organization and its products and services. This is a medium about uniqueness and personality. Only the companies that figure that out will be able to work in this medium effectively.

FRED WILF

Fred Wilf is special counsel practicing technology and electronic property law at Saul, Ewing, Remick & Saul in Berwyn, Pennsylvania. He has been studying online law for several years, and also has hosted regular online forums on commercial online services. His view of the Web focuses on legal ramifications for businesses that suddenly find themselves crossing global boundaries:

> *Every time there's a new communications medium, businesses, especially small businesses, learn quickly how to adapt the new medium to make money. That was true of telegrams, the telephone, and recently has been true of email and the Web. I expect this to continue, and that means there will be tremendous opportunity and lots of risk. It will take a while for the law to catch up to some of these issues. For example, when is an online contract made? And when can it be enforced? Who is responsible for making sure that a message arrives at its destination unchanged? The telephone and telegraph issues took ten years or more to work themselves out, but I think these online issues will only take a year or two to settle down. The courts are more willing to be open-minded to the issues of new technology than they were then.*
>
> *To a certain extent the online world is already regulated. We'll see a lot of attempts to apply different legal approaches to the Web—do we treat it as if it were a phone line? Or do we apply the law of hard copy publishing and treat it as if it were a magazine or newspaper? The answer will be that you have to look at what the Web is doing. Some concepts apply in different ways. I expect we'll see more regulation of how online commerce is done. Electronic Data Interchange law will be applied, and existing laws on email.*
>
> *The Web is indeed worldwide, and most U.S. laws simply don't apply. That includes little things like the Constitution. Foreign countries insist that companies doing business on the Web abide by foreign law, and those cases will become higher profile. I expect that each country that wants to control Web content for any reason will continue to block access to sites. Most likely those will be sites with anything the least bit sexual or political. Don't expect the First Amendment to apply because there isn't one outside the United States. Anyone in the United States who sells in Europe and causes problems may be liable for criminal infringement in Europe. Before you provide services or goods across the Web to countries you haven't done business with before, research them. Europe has laws and expects you to abide by them.*

Even the fact that the Web crosses state lines can become an issue. The Thomas case was a real warning about that. The Thomases ran an X-rated bulletin board service based in California, and what they were doing was okay by California standards. But people were accessing it in Tennessee and the Thomases knew that. So they were subjected to and prosecuted under Tennessee law. Businesses that have features like Web chat will be similarly responsible for activity on their sites. If someone is at the site and going over the edge in any way, and the Webmaster knows about it, he or she may be held liable if anything happens thereafter.

Appendix 1

•••••••••••

Getting Online and Browsing Around

Central Source Yellow Page
www.telephonebook.com
Free
Enormous database of company names, addresses, and telephone numbers from the yellow pages published throughout America.

Internet Service Providers Directory
www.commerce.net:80/directories/products/isp/
Lists links to Internet service providers by geographic area and name.

The List
www.thelist.com
Lists Internet service providers across the country, organized by zip code into a searchable database.

Web Review Magazine
www.gnn.com/wr
Free
Online magazine published weekly and updated daily that provides insights into the people, places, technology, and issues of the Web. Its features and in-depth reviews instruct the user where to best spend his or her time on the Web.

SOFTWARE

For Individual Computers

All-in-One Internet Kit
Wentworth Worldwide Media
1866 Colonial Village Lane
Lancaster, PA 17605
800-638-1639
www.classroom.net
$59
Offers full access to the Internet. The Web browser and mail clients are licensed versions of NetManage's proprietary Internet Chameleon.

Emissary Desktop
Attachmate
1129 San Antonio Road
Palo Alto, CA 94303
800-872-8649
www.attachmate.com
$149
Users can send mail, copy files, access remote applications, keep up on news, and browse the World Wide Web from this Windows application. Emissary's object-based applications layers handle all the Internet's foreign protocols and data formats automatically.

Explore 2.0
FTP Software
100 Brickstone Square, 5th Floor
Andover, MA 01810
800-282-4387
www.ftp.com
$49.99
Software that can search the Internet for information, send and receive E-mail, read and participate in newsgroups, or browse the Web for the latest entertainment, stock quotes, or news. Explore is aimed at small businesses, telecommuters, and home PC enthusiasts who want to become more productive on the Internet and communicate with enterprise networks.

IBM Internet Connection for Windows 4.0
IBM
Dept. G90, P.O. Box 12195
Research Triangle Park, NC 27709
800-342-6672
$39
www.ibm.com
IBM's Internet application suite developed for the home and small-business community. Automatic access and easy installation. The software includes World Wide Web access with WebExplorer, its newsgroup and email software.

Internet Anywhere
Open Text
180 Columbia Street West
Waterloo, ONT N2L 3L3
Canada
519-888-9910
www.opentext.com
$79
A suite of Internet tools wrapped together in one easy-to-use, integrated, and customizable desktop. Everything users need to access and work on the Internet.

Internet Chameleon and Internet Chameleon for Windows
Netmanage Inc.
10725 N. DeAnza Boulevard
Cupertino, CA 95014
408-973-7171
www.netmanage.com
$125 single user, $1,250 for 10 users; Windows version is $495
Complete Internet connection kit with many tools. Suite of 48 individual applications including Internet access, host connectivity, email, group collaboration, and desktop management. Newtshooter shares information among applications.

Internet in a Box
Compuserve Internet Division (Spry)
316 Occidental Avenue South, Suite 200
Seattle, WA 98104
800-848-8990
www.spry.com
$149, single copy

An all-in-one package for connecting to the Internet and Compuserve using SLIP or PPP from a Windows PC. Includes Secure Mosaic, newsreader, Telnet, FTP, Gopher, and POP mail transfer.

Internet Made Easy
U.S. Online Inc.
2445 152nd Avenue NE
Redmond, WA 98052
206-867-5103
www.usonline.com
$69.95
Internet productivity software. Recommends which online service is most appropriate and cost-effective for a user's personal interests. A user profile is established, and Internet Made Easy automatically retrieves and presents information most relevant to each user.

InternetSuite for Windows
Quarterdeck Corporation
13160 Mindano Way, 3rd Floor
Marina del Rey, CA 90292
800-354-3222
www.qdeck.com
$39.95
Includes Quarterdeck Mosaic World Wide Web browser. Quarterdeck Message Center offers full email and usenet newsgroup capability. Quarterdeck File Transfer Protocol allows users to copy and transfer files to others. QTerm (telnet) lets users access a remote computer from anywhere in the world.

Mosaic
www.ncsa.uiuc.edu/SDG/Software/Mosaic/NCSAMosaicHome.html
Free
NCSA Mosaic is the first graphical Web browser software, copyrighted by the Board of Trustees of the University of Illinois (UI). UI grants users a license without a fee to use the Mosaic software for personal, academic, research, government, and internal business purposes. It is available for Macintosh, MS Windows (3.1x, 95, and NT), and X-Windows.

NetCruiser
Netcom Online Communications Services Inc.
3031 Tisch Way
San Jose, CA 95128

800-353-6600
www.netcom.com
$25 setup; $19.95 monthly
Point-and-click Internet access to Netcom. Setup is user-friendly. Includes common Internet tools such as Web browser, news, email, and Gopher.

PowerBrowser
Oracle
500 Oracle Parkway
Redwood Shores, CA 94065
800-672-2531
www.oracle.com
Free (demo version)
PowerBrowser can display "applets" written in the Java programming language. These applets can make standard Web pages come alive by adding live animation and greater user interactivity with the operating system. Power-Browser currently runs on Windows 3.1x, Windows 95, and Windows NT. PowerBrowser also includes a Web server and an Authoring Wizard to let users quickly create your first Web pages.

SuperHighway Access
Frontier Technologies Corporation
10201 N. Port Washington Road
Mequon, WI 53092
414-241-4555
SuperHighway@FrontierTech.com
$89
Fully integrated Internet access product that combines friendly interfaces with functionality. Utilities include browser, Gopher, WAIS, CSO phone book, email, newsreader, and Telnet.

WebCompass
Quarterdeck Corporation
13160 Mindano Way, 3rd Floor
Marina del Rey, CA 90292
800-354-3222
www.qdeck.com
$99
Windows program allows users to conduct a search using several Web search engines simultaneously with a single query. Users can schedule WebCompass

to query selected Web sites in the background, automatically updating their database with new information on topics of interest.

World Wide Web Kit
Ventana Media
P.O. Box 2468
Chapel Hill, NC 27515
919-942-0220
www.vmedia.com
$49.95

Contains an array of software, documentation, and interactive technology, including Netscape Navigator. Includes a CD Accelerator, which allows users to access up-to-date information online while pulling high-bandwidth images and multimedia from the CD-ROM, adding speed to Web traveling.

For Networks

Cyber Sentry
Microsystems Software
600 Worcester Road
Framingham, MA 01701
508-879-9000
www.microsys.com

Cyber Patrol for consumers is $49.95; Cyber Sentry for corporate users is $695 for 50 users, and up to $1,295 for 250 users

Windows-based software allowing administrators to specify categories to be blocked by content, time of day, or site.

Distinct TCP/IP for Windows
Distinct Corporation
14395 Saratoga Avenue, Suite 120
Saratoga, CA 95070
408-366-8933
www.distinct.com
$395

Allows users to manage Telnet sessions, email and file transfers using multi-tasking capabilities.

Explore Anywhere
FTP Software

100 Brickstone Square, 5th Floor
Andover, MA 01810
800-282-4387
www.ftp.com
$199
Designed for workgroups, telecommuters, and small businesses that want to explore the Internet from anywhere—home, office, airport, or hotel room. Whether working on a LAN, using a modem, or switching between both, Explore Anywhere delivers the network connectivity and all the easy-to-use applications to explore the entire Internet.

Internet Office
CompuServe Internet Division (Spry)
316 Occidental Avenue South, Suite 200
Seattle, WA 98104
800-777-9638
www.spry.com
Four editions: Premier, $499; Professional, $399; Navigator, $199; and Mosaic, $49.95
A fully featured suite of Internet applications aimed at business customers, especially users accessing the Internet from a local area network (LAN). Allows users to access their corporate network and Internet resources from any location in the U.S. as if they were dialing locally. Includes the latest version of CompuServe's WinCim.

Internet WatchDog
Algorithm Inc.
11660 Alpharetta Highway, Suite 265
Roswell, GA 30076
770-751-5801
www.algorithm.com
$29.95
Allows the administrator to track what tasks are performed on employee's terminals. Stores a log of every important computer event of the user—when the computer was turned on, software used, and when used, etc.

RUMBA for the Internet
Wall Data, Inc.
11332 N.E. 122nd Way
Kirkland, WA 98034

206-814-9255
www.walldata.com
$150 per user
For users of RUMBA Office. RUMBA for the Internet adds low-cost Internet access. Also provides navigation and communications applications, Gopher, and RUMBA Air News for browsing, and posting to Usenet news groups.

WebTrack
Webster Network Strategies
1100 5th Avenue South, Suite 307
Naples, FL 33940
941-261-5503
www.webster.com
$495 for 1 to 5 users; up to $11,995 for unlimited users
Lets corporations provide employees with Internet access while restricting entry to unwanted Internet sites. Software enables businesses to restrict access to any of fifteen categories of Internet sites containing pornography, gambling, merchandising, illegal drugs, hate speech, criminal skills, sports, job searching, personal pages, alternative journals, entertainment, games, and humor. An occurrence prompts the software to shut down the monitor, application, or system and make a note of the breach on its audit trail.

For Both Individual Computers and Networks

The Internet Adapter (TIA)
InterMind Corp
1101 N. Northlake Way, Suite 106
Seattle, WA 98103
206-545-7565
www.intermind.com
$25 for single user; $495 for 250 shell users
Allows users to transform a text-based Internet shell account into a graphics-based, dialup IP connection.

Mariner
FTP Software
2953 Bunker Hill Lane, Suite 400
Santa Clara, CA 95054
800-282-4387
www.ftp.com
$99

Windows-based Internet tool that groups applications under one interface, including World Wide Web, email, newsgroups, Internet relay chat, FTP, Gopher, and Telnet.

Morning Star PPP
Morning Star Technologies
1760 Zollinger Road, Suite 420
Columbus, OH 43221
800-558-7827
synergy.smartpages.com/mstar
$795; $400 if purchased for connecting to the Internet
UNIX-based system designed to provide users with reliable communication software that can be used as either a client or server for TCP/IP connectivity. Interoperates with most Internet connectivity providers.

Navigator
Netscape Corporation
501 E. Middlefield Road
Mountain View, CA 94043
800-638-7483
www.netscape.com
$39 for individual users
Personal edition of the popular browser software. Includes the full capabilities of the original LAN edition, full email capabilities, easy Internet access, and remote connectivity capabilities.

PC/TCP
FTP Software
2 High Street
North Andover, MA 01845
800-282-4387
info@ftp.com
Call for pricing
Designed to allow users to easily access network resources. Terminal emulation, FTP, network file sharing, network utilities, and more.

Super-TCP for Windows
Frontier Technologies Corporation
10201 N. Port Washington Road
Mequon, WI 53092
414-241-4555
www.frontiertech.com

$395

TCP/IP connectivity for Windows. Features a Telnet command, an FTP command, an FTP server, and a mail system.

INTERNET SERVICE PROVIDERS

America Online
8619 Westwood Center Drive
Vienna, VA 22182
800-827-6364
Ten free hours, then $9.95 monthly for up to five hours of usage. Each additional hour is $2.95.
The largest and fastest-growing provider of online services in the world, with 3.5 million subscribers. AOL offers Web site development and hosting capability to subscribers. Offers Internet access via Netscape, Microsoft's Web browser, and AOL's own proprietary browser.

CompuServe
5000 Arlington Center Boulevard
Columbus, OH 43220
800-848-8199
www.sprynet.com
$9.95 per month for the first five hours; $2.95 for each additional hour.
This business-oriented service was the first commercial online service. Internet access is offered more cheaply through CompuServe's Sprynet division.

Prodigy
445 Hamilton Avenue
White Plains, NY 10601
800-776-3449
www.prodigy.com
$9.95 per month for the first five hours; $2.95 for each additional hour.
This consumer-oriented online service was the first to offer access to the Web.

PSINet
510 Huntmar Park Drive
Herndon, VA 22070

800-827-7482

www.psi.net

$19.95–$4,000 per month, depending upon level of service.

PSINet provides a wide variety of Internet solutions for small and large businesses, ranging from entry-level dialup access to high-speed dedicated leased line attachments. Also offers security and Web site hosting services.

Sprynet

CompuServe Internet Division (Spry)

316 Occidental Avenue South, Suite 200

Seattle, WA 98104

800-848-8990

www.compuserve.com

Unlimited Internet access $19.95; 3 hours, $4.95; 7 hours, $9.95

Users can use any software browser and sign up it from Sprynet's Web site. The signup package offers both Microsoft Internet Explorer and Netscape Navigator. The service offers local dialup access from more than 480 points of presence (local phone numbers) worldwide.

UUNET Technologies

3060 Williams Drive

Fairfax, VA 22031-4648

800-488-6384

www.uu.net

$25 activation fee plus $30 for 25 hours of access, $2 for each additional hour. National Internet service provider offering PPP accounts for accessing the Web.

PUBLICATIONS

Internet Roadside Attractions (including CD-ROM) by Gareth Branwyn

Ventana Press, Inc.

P.O. Box 2468

Chapel Hill, NC 27515

919-942-0220

www.vmedia.com

$29.95

Guide to Internet sites, includes Mac or Windows format CD-ROM. Book includes an alphabetically categorized list of sites.

The Internet Yellow Pages
Osborne/McGraw-Hill
2600 10th Street
Berkeley, CA 94710
510-549-0600
osborne.mhs.compuserve.com
$29.95
This best-selling reference to the Internet is in its third edition.

Official World Wide Web Yellow Pages
New Riders (an imprint of Macmillan Computer Publishing)
201 W. 103rd Street
Indianapolis, IN 46290
800-428-5331
www.mcp.com
$29.99
Comprehensive source for finding information via the World Wide Web, listing more than 8,000 sites and resources. Includes a topical map, subject finder, index, and numerous cross references.

Walking the World Wide Web by Shannon Turlington
Ventana Press, Inc.
P.O. Box 2468
Chapel Hill, NC 27515
919-942-0220
www.vmedia.com
$29.95
This guide to the Web includes several sites to browse on an introductory CD-ROM with Ventana Mosaic Web browser software.

The World Wide Web Complete Reference by Rick Stout
Osborne/McGraw-Hill
2600 10th Street
Berkeley, CA 94710
510-549-0600
osborne.mhs.compuserve.com
$29.95
Complete reference to the Web, including getting connected, using browsers, creating Web pages, and creating HTML documents, among other topics.

The World Wide Web Unleashed by John December and Neil Randall
Sams Publishing (a Macmillan imprint)
201 W. 103rd Street
Indianapolis, IN 46290
317-581-3500
$35.00
This comprehensive directory includes information on how to connect to the
Web and where to go, as well as illustrations of Web sites.

Firewalls

SOFTWARE/HARDWARE

Black Hole
Milkyway Networks Corporation
2055 Gateway Place, Suite 400
San Jose, CA 95110
408-467-3868
www.milkyway.com
Starts at $2,900 for ten users
Second-generation, application-level firewall. Attempts at hacking are
detected with the blanketed network monitoring feature, and organizations can
create a virtual private network using DES-based data encryption feature. No
restriction on the use of applications such as email, Gopher, and Mosaic
because of full security for all TCP-IP applications.

CyberGuard 2.0
Harris Computer Systems Corp.
2101 West Cypress Creek Road
Fort Lauderdale, FL 33309
305-974-1700
www.hcsc.com
$25,000
New version includes added software and hardware security, Internet Protocol
address masking and translations, and increased performance. CyberGuard
hides from the Internet the IP addresses of machines inside the corporate
network. Designed to prevent someone from spoofing a known IP address to
gain entry.

Eagle Firewall
Raptor Systems, Inc.
69 Hickory Drive
Waltham, MA 02154
617-487-7700
www.raptor.com
1 to 50 users, $7,000; 1 to 200 users, $15,000; unlimited users, $25,000
An application-level firewall that combines comprehensive access controls
with real-time monitoring and suspicious activity detection to protect against
unauthorized Internet access. Runs on the three major UNIX platforms (Sun,
HP, and IBM workstations).

EagleNomad
Raptor Systems, Inc.
69 Hickory Drive
Waltham, MA 02154
617-487-7700
www.raptor.com
$99
Firewall product line designed to give roaming PC users access via the Internet
to corporate files while protecting the company's sensitive data. Includes
portable PC security with three-time password accounts and authorization
code. Users have the option of encrypting sent and received data files.

Entrust
Northern Telecom (Nortel)
Entrust Sales
Dept. D700, Mailstop 505, WDLN
P.O. Box 3511, Station C
Ottawa, ONT K1Y 4H7
Canada
800-4NORTEL
$159 per user license
www.nortel.com
Data security software that includes support for Macintosh and UNIX operat-
ing systems. Cross-platform public key infrastructure product that scales to
tens of thousands of users. Software can be used internationally.

FireWall-1
CheckPoint Software Technologies, Inc.
One Militia Drive

Lexington, MA 02173

800-429-4391

www.checkpoint.com

$4,990 to $18,900, depending on number of users

Provides integrated, secure support for all network activities, including electronic commerce and RealAudio.

Gauntlet Internet Firewall

Mergent International, Inc.

70 Inwood Road

Rocky Hill, CT 06067

860-257-4223

www.mergent.com

$15,000 turney, includes hardware, software, installation, training; $11,000 for software, installation, and training only.

Hardware- and software-based firewall system to provide secure access and internetwork communication between private and public networks. An application-level gateway between IP networks. Version 3.0 includes commercial quality documentation, management tools, reporting tools, "smoke alarms," completely transparent proxies, firewall-to-firewall encryption, protection from "IP Spoofing" attacks, and full commercial support.

NET1-FireWall

Network-1

909 Third Avenue, 9th Floor

New York, NY 10022

800-638-9751

www.network-1.com

$11,900

Combines hardware and software to block traffic to a system unless the user is enabled by the network administrator. Features frame and packet filtering for more than 400 preconfigured protocols and dynamic packet filtering. Hardware consists of a 486 PC with 16MB of memory, a 500MB hard disk, a 3.5-inch floppy drive, and two network controllers.

Private Internet Exchange

Network Translation, Inc.

2464 Embarcadero Road

Palo Alto, CA 94303

415-842-2100

www.translation.com

Software provides full firewall protection without the administrative overhead and risks associated with UNIX-based firewall systems. The network administrator is provided with a complete accounting and logging of all transactions, including attempted break-ins.

SecureConnect
Morning Star Technologies, Inc.
3518 Riverside Drive, Suite 101
Columbus, OH 43221
800-558-7827
www.morningstar.com
$1,495
Software for UNIX; combines Morning Star's Internet standard point-to-point software with its advanced dynamic firewall packet filtering and virtual private networking technology. Dynamic packet filtering technology adapts its structure during execution to open, time, and lock the port needed for a transaction, providing maximum network security.

Sidewinder
Secure Computing Corp.
2675 Longlake Road
Roseville, MN 55113
800-692-LOCK
www.sidewinder.com
$30,000
Provides both Internet services and server security software. It senses intruders, sounds a silent alarm, and then allows the administrator to terminate the user, provide misleading information, or identify the user for future prosecution.

SmartGate
Virtual Open Network Environment Corporation (V-ONE)
1803 Research Boulevard, Suite 305
Rockville, MD 20850
301-838-8900
techweb.cmp.com/cw
$10,000
A network security product. Through client/server hardware and software, users can create a secure channel over the Internet to transfer information and financial transactions. Includes a Pentium-based PC platform with a UNIX

operating system, an authentication server, Data Encryption Standard encryption, and TCP/IP application that operate with existing database, Telnet, and electronic mail applications.

PUBLICATIONS

Computer Crime: A Crimefighter's Handbook by David Icove, Karl Seger, and William VonStorch
O'Reilly & Associates, Inc.
103 Morris Street, Suite A
Sebastopol, CA 95472
800-998-9938
www.ora.com
$24.95
Easy to understand, this book covers firewalls for non-technical readers.

Building Internet Firewalls by D. Brent Chapman and Elizabeth D. Zwicky
O'Reilly & Associates, Inc.
103 Morris Street, Suite A
Sebastopol, CA 95472
800-998-9938
www.ora.com
$29.95
A practical guide to protecting computer systems from the growing threats to Internet security. Describes a variety of firewall approaches and architectures.

Appendix 2
● ● ● ● ● ● ● ● ● ● ● ●

Designing and Developing
a Web Site

ColorServe Info Page
www.biola.edu/cgi-bin/colorserve/colorserve.html
Lets visitors pick and view different background colors online, providing users
with the hexidecimal code needed to add to their HTML code.

"HTML Overview," an excerpt from *Managing Internet Information Services,*
by Cricket Liu
O'Reilly & Associates
103 Morris Street, Suite A
Sebastopol, CA 95472
800-998-9938
www.ora.com
Free
Sixteen-page downloadable article that discusses document structure, HTML
tag syntax, creating hyperlinks, and dealing with graphics.

The Interactive Graphics Renderer Page
www.eece.ksu.edu/IGRNEW
Simple interface allows visitors to create and download customized graphics,
including icons, buttons, and lines.

The VRML Repository
www.sdsc.edu/vrml
This comprehensive site offers information on virtual reality modeling language, where to get the software, and how to use it.

SOFTWARE

askSam Electronic Publisher
askSam Systems
P.O. Box 1428
Perry, FL 32347
904-584-6590
www.asksam.com
Standard single user, $149.95; professional version for larger files, $395
The Web Publisher puts full-text searchable documents and databases on the Internet without programming or HTML codes. The Web Publisher runs on all Windows NT 3.51 and Windows 95 Web servers.

Asymetrix Web 3D
Asymetrix Corporation
110-110 Avenue NE
Bellevue, WA 98004
800-448-6543
www.asymetrix.com
$179
Enables user to create three-dimensional graphics for a home page from the desktop. Can be used to convert images to GIF and other standard Internet formats, and then connect the design to a URL with an HTML editor.

Common Ground Web Publishing System
Common Ground Software
303 Twin Dolphin Drive, Suite 420
Redwood City, CA 94065
415-802-5800
info@commonground.com
$999
Complements HTML for creating, publishing, and distributing fully formatted documents over the Internet.

Cyberleaf 1.0
Interleaf, Inc.
62 Fourth Avenue
Waltham, MA 02154
617-290-0710
www.ileaf.com
$1,595
HTML conversion tool.

FrontPage
Vermeer Technologies
725 Concord Avenue, 6th Floor
Cambridge, MA 02138
800-932-0075
www.vermeer.com
Free
Runs on Windows. Has sophisticated features for mapping out an entire Web site, giving user a graphical view of all the pages, and showing links that aren't yet connected to subsequent pages.

HotDog Editor
Sausage Software
P.O. Box 36
Briar Hill 3088
Australia
www.sausage.com
Shareware fee: standard edition $29.95; pro edition $79.95
Guides user through the process of creating documents that the user can publish on the Web. Includes ways to easily incorporate HTML 1.0, 2.0, and many of the proposed HTML version 3.0 features into user's online creations.

HoTMetaL Pro
SoftQuad Inc.
56 Aberfoyle Crescent, Suite 810
Toronto, ONT M8X 2W4
Canada
416-239-4801
www.sq.com
$199
Publishing tool; includes templates, dialog box support for linking to other documents, spell checking, thesaurus, context-sensitive search and replace,

flexible stylesheets, and an importing feature that cleans up and converts invalid HTML documents. Conforms to SGML (Standard Generalized Markup Language), the international standard for information exchange.

HTML 3.0
www.hpl.hp.co.uk/people/dsr/html/CoverPage.html
Free
Gives Web publishers greater control over their content. Documents will have the capacity to be richer and have more interactive applications. Tags in HTML 3.0 will make the process of putting tables on Web sites more automated. Publishers will also be able to add captions to displayed images.

HTML Transit
InfoAccess, Inc.
2800 156th Avenue SE
Bellevue, WA 98007
206-747-3203
www.infoaccess.com
$495
Employs a template-based architecture to automatically generate HTML publications using source files from any major word processor.

InContext Spider
InContext Corporation
6701 Democracy Boulevard, Suite 300
Bethesda, MD 20817
301-571-9464
www.incontext.com
$99
Web authoring software that works behind the scenes to ensure that every Web document created complies with HTML's many rules. It helps build a Web page every step of the way, telling users what can be inserted in specific locations and when.

Internet Assistant for Word
Microsoft Corporation
One Microsoft Way
Redmond, WA 98052
800-426-9400
www.microsoft.com
Free

High-end authoring tool for HTML documents that works with Microsoft Word.

Internet Creator
Forman Interactive
201 Water Street
Brooklyn, NY 11201-1174
718-522-2260
www.forman.com
$189
Windows-based software combined with one free month of Web server space; allows creation and publishing of Web pages, including options and designs for custom tailoring.

Internet Publishing Kit
Ventana Communications Group
P.O. Box 2468
Chapel Hill, NC 27515
919-942-0220
www.vmedia.com
$129
Windows and Macintosh kit contains tools for creating Web documents.

Java
Sun Microsystems
2550 Garcia Avenue
Mountain View, CA 94043-1100
800-786-2441
www.java.sun.com/JDK-1.0
Free
This early version of Web design language allows programmers to build special effects into Web sites. Not recommended for beginners.

JetForm Filler
JetForm Corporation
7600 Leesburg Pike, East Bldg., Suite 430
Falls Church, VA 22043
703-448-9544
www.jetform.com
$149

New version of the company's electronic forms software that can be used to fill out "intelligent" forms embedded in Web pages. These forms can perform calculations automatically or prevent the wrong type of information from being entered into a field.

NaviPress
NaviSoft Inc.
8619 Westwood Center Drive
Vienna, VA 22182
703-918-2533
www.navisoft.com
Free
Downloadable Web authoring software that allows table creation; runs on Windows, Macintosh, and Sun/UNIX.

NetCarta WebMapper
NetCarta Corporation
5617 Scotts Valley Drive, Suite 100
Scotts Valley, CA 95066
408-461-8920
www.netcarta.com
$500
Allows Webmasters to analyze, manage, navigate, and organize their sites.

net.Form 2.0
NetGenesis Corporation
68 Rogers Street
Cambridge, MA 02142
617-577-9800
www.netgen.com
$495
Automated form processing engine; features open database connectivity.

Netscape Secure Commerce Server
Netscape Communications
501 East Middlefield Road
Mountain View, CA 94043
415-254-1900
$5,000
www.netscape.com

Netscape's server software for creating business sites. Offers secure transaction capability to visitors using Netscape's browser software.

net.Thread
NetGenesis Corporation
68 Rogers Street
Cambridge, MA 02142
617-577-9800
www.netgen.com
$1,495 for UNIX; $895 for Windows NT
Allows users to create and manage Web chat forums.

Open Inventor
Template Graphics Software, Inc.
9920 Pacific Heights Boulevard, Suite 200
San Diego, CA 92121
619-457-5359
www.sd.tgs.com/~template
$995
Cross-platform product using C++ 3-D graphics application development; works on Windows 95.

PageMill
Adobe Systems Inc.
1585 Charleston Road
Mountain View, CA 94039
415-961-4400
www.adobe.com
$99 (downloadable)
Authoring tool for Macintosh. Allows nontechnical users to create pages with transparent GIFs, forms, and background images. Easy to manipulate text and graphics.

Panorama
SoftQuad, Inc.
56 Aberfoyle Crescent, Suite 810
Toronto, ONT M8X 2W4
Canada
www.sq.com
416-239-4801
Free with purchase of latest version of NCSA Mosaic; $195 list price

Displays Computer Graphics Metafile images of technical illustration in electronic documents. Standard Generalized Markup Language (SGML) browsing technology. SGML supports the creation of longer and more complex documents than previously available on the Web.

Step Search
Saqqara
1230 Oakmead Parkway, Suite 314
Sunnyvale, CA 94086
408-738-4858
www.saqqara.com
$695
Graphical search and compare mechanism, enables companies to systematically guide customers through the features and benefits of a product line and serves as an online sales guide. Works with any Internet browser.

Swift 2.0
NetManage
10725 North De Anza Boulevard
Cupertino, CA 95014
408-973-7171
www.netmanage.com
$199 single copy
This server software is based on NetManage's Chameleon applications. Can be used to create and maintain on Intranet or Web site.

WebAuthor
Quarterdeck Corporation
13160 Mindano Way, 3rd Floor
Marina del Rey, CA 90292
800-354-3222
www.qdeck.com
$149.95
Works within Microsoft Word for Windows.

Web Publisher
SkiSoft Publishing Corporation
1644 Massachusetts Avenue, Suite 79
Lexington, MA 02173
617-863-1876
www.skisoft.com

$495; professional edition, $990
Windows-based software that converts documents created in Word, WordPer-fect, Excel, or Frame into HTML.

WebSite
O'Reilly & Associates
103 Morris Street, Suite A
Sebastopol, CA 95472
800-998-9938
www.ora.com
$379
Windows NT- and Windows 95-based server software, that includes an HTML editor and multiple search indexes.

WebSuite
DigitalStyle Corporation
16885 Via del Campo Court, Suite 202
San Diego, CA 92127
619-673-5050
www.digitalstyle.com
Starter edition $199; standard edition, $299; designer edition, $529
Web design and implementation software combining text and graphics.

Web Whiz
Ocean State Publishing Corporation
P.O. Box 747
Woonsocket, RI 02895
401-767-3376
www.RISoftSystems.com
$24.95
CD-ROM tool for designing home pages. Contains more than 2,000 graphics files plus two professional HTML editors, two Web browsers, and hypertext HTML reference materials.

PUBLICATIONS

HTML Publishing on the Internet (with CD-ROM toolkit) by Brent Heslop and Larry Budnick
Ventana Press

P.O. Box 2468
Chapel Hill, NC 27515
919-942-0220
www.vmedia.com
$49.95
This step-by-step guide to creating a Web site using basic HTML software comes with a CD-ROM that includes HotMetal Pro editing software, Netscape Navigator, and other helpful packages.

The Internet Business Kit
John Wiley & Sons Publishers
605 Third Avenue
New York, NY 10158
800-850-6000
www.wiley.com
$69.95
A CD-ROM and two-book set. Includes software and instructions to open an Internet account, set up a Web page, use email, take orders, conduct market research, etc. Includes the publications *Marketing on the Internet* and *The Internet Business Book.*

Weaving the Internal Corporate Web by Tammy Lowe
Osborne
800-722-4726
$29.95
This step-by-step guide shows how to create an internal Web site to meet the needs of different types of companies.

Web Developer magazine
Mecklermedia Corporation
20 Ketchum Street
Westport, CT 06880
203-341-2842
www.iworld.com
$21 per year
Magazine for Internet programmers, Webmasters, network administrators, and other technically oriented personnel responsible for developing and maintaining software, hardware, and security on Web sites.

The Web Page Design Cookbook by William Horton, Lee Taylor, Arthur Ignacio, and Nancy Hoft

John Wiley & Sons, Inc.
605 Third Avenue
New York, NY 10158
212-850-6000
www.wiley.com
$34.95
Guide to creating Web pages. Design tips, style elements, tips on international design, and answers to frequently asked questions.

Appendix 3
• • • • • • • • • • •

Maintaining and Promoting
a Web Site

Maintaining a Web Site

SOFTWARE

Alpha Server
Comport Consulting Corporation
249 Goffle Road
Hawthorne, NJ 07506
201-427-3500
E-mail address: info@comport.com
$544
Internet connectivity hardware server bundle with pre-installed Internet software.

CyberWeb
Tandem Computers, Inc.
14050 Summit Drive
Austin, TX 78728
800-826-3367
www.tandem.com
Packages from $1,068 to $12,000
Family of products built on open architecture, capable of supporting a full range
of Web clients, server software, security protocols and development tools. Built

on the company's fault-tolerant computers, specifically designed to handle large volumes of transactions.

Merchant Solution
Open Market, Inc.
245 First Street
Cambridge, MA 02142
617-621-9500
www.openmarket.com
Package starts at $19,995
A bundled software/service program for companies looking to do online business. WebServer product handles tasks such as displaying product brochures or catalogs and logging order information from Web-surfing customers. A company would then contract for the service portion of Merchant Solution to process incoming orders through Open Market's headquarters.

Netscape Secure Commerce Server (See page 197.)

Spry SafetyWeb Server
CompuServe
3535 128th Avenue, SE
Bellevue, WA 98006
www.spry.com
$1,295
Web server software; includes open database connectivity and allows remote administration of a Web site via Windows 95 or Windows NT.

VRServer
WebMaster, Inc.
1601 Civic Center Drive, Suite 200
Santa Clara, CA 95050
408-345-1800
www.webmaster.com
$249
Takes data written in HTML and converts it to Virtual Reality Modeling Language (VRML).

WebChat Server Software
WebChat Communications
1030 Curtis Street
Menlo Park, CA 94025

415-327-4386
wbs.net/wcc.html
Product is $3,000 for up to 50 users; service is $595 per month for up to 50 users
Allows users to either buy software or rent space on WebChat's server for live Web chat.

WebSite Server
O'Reilly & Associates Inc.
103 Morris Street, Suite A
Sebastopol, CA 95472
800-998-9938
www.ora.com
$499
Designed to turn mainstream PCs, running a consumer-oriented operating system, into full-fledged Web hosts.

PUBLICATIONS

How to Set Up and Maintain a World Wide Web Site by Lincoln D. Stein
Addison-Wesley Publishing Company
One Jacob Way
Reading, MA 01867
617-944-3700
$29
Following every stage of the process, this book covers all aspects of Web site design, setup, and maintenance, including sections on working with sound, graphics, and video.

The Web Server Book (with CD-ROM toolkit) by Jonathan Magid, R. Douglas Matthews, and Paul Jones
Ventana Press Inc.
P.O. Box 2468
Chapel Hill, NC 27515
919-942-0220
www.vmedia.com
$49.95
This illustrated guide includes a companion CD-ROM with server software.

Promoting a Web Site

ADnet
www.addnet.com
$25 per month for 6 months
ADnet will design and publish a customized three-page Web site for user's business. ADnet will then register links to that page on a variety of popular servers and monitor the page's performance with daily usage statistics.

Alta Vista
www.altavista.digital.com
The most comprehensive search engine, Alta Vista lists keyword matches from among nearly every Web site and Usenet newsgroups. Even if companies don't register with Alta Vista, the search engine's software will eventually find the site and include it in the listings.

InfoSeek
www2.infoseek.com
Searches and browses from among Web pages, Usenet newsgroups, and FTP and Gopher sites.

InterNIC
www.ds.internic.net
Herndon, VA
703-742-4777
Registers and stores all Internet domain names.

Lycos
www.lycos.com
A complete guide to the Internet, including a directory of the most popular sites, critical reviews of the Web's top sites, real-time news links, and on-target editorial content.

Open Text
www.opentext.com
Open Text's full text indexing software power-searches the World Wide Web for company sites.

Promote-It!
www.cam.org/~psarena/promote-it.html

Free

A compilation of the Net's publicity tools. Submits URL and site description to dozens of search engines, newsgroups, and mailing lists at one time.

Smart Site

www.smart-site.com

Fee-based marketing service for publicizing Web sites

Submit It!

submit-it.permalink.com/submit-it/

Free

Distributes a company's Web site information into several different search engines.

Webcrawler

www.webcrawler.com

Operated by the commercial online service America Online, Webcrawler offers a high-quality, fast, and free Internet search service for businesses that list with the site.

Yahoo!

www.yahoo.com

The Web's first search engine, Yahoo! lists sites only after editors review them and decide that they offer useful content.

PUBLICATIONS

CyberMarketing by Len Keeler

Amacom

135 West 50th Street

New York, NY 10020

212-586-8100

$24.95

Offers tips on marketing to the entire Internet, including using newsgroups, email, and commercial online services.

Guerrilla Marketing Online by Jay Conrad Levinson and Charles Rubin

Houghton-Mifflin

215 Park Avenue South

New York, NY 10003

212-420-5800

$12.95

This book applies Levinson's popular small business marketing strategies to the Web.

Marketing on the Internet by Jill Ellsworth and Matthew Ellsworth
John Wiley & Sons
605 Third Avenue
New York, NY 10158-0012
212-850-6768
$24.95

Focuses on how to design usable Web sites; filled with illustrations of real Web pages.

Marketing on the Internet by Michael Mathiesen
Maximum Press
605 Silverthorn Road
Gulf Breeze, FL 32561
904-934-0819
$39.95

The twelve-step plan outlined in the book covers the commercial online services as well. Comes with Spry Mosaic software.

The Small Business Guide to Internet Marketing by Al Bredenberg
Al Bredenberg Business Reports
Cornwall, CT 06753
800-843-4272
www.copywriter.com/ab/
$11.20

E-mailed guide available directly from the author. Includes tips to help Internet business users avoid making some of the common mistakes of Internet marketing.

Appendix 4

•••••••••••

Tracking Uisitors and Processing Transactions

Tracking Visitors

SOFTWARE

Intersé market focus
Intersé Corporation
65 North Ivandale
Hamilton, VA 22068
703-759-4375
info@interse.com
Entry pricing at $300 per month
Standard software package for tracking visitor rates. Includes information requested, number of requests, full company names, peak viewing times, etc. Publicizes a company's Web server address on all appropriate Internet lists and newsgroups.

NetAnalysis
NetGenesis Corporation
68 Rogers Street
Cambridge, MA 02142
617-577-9800
www.netgen.com

$2,995

Allows Web site operators to track traffic to the site. Can reveal whether visitors come from commercial or educational accounts and what time of day they are most likely to visit.

Personal Web Site
W3.COM
459 Hamilton Avenue
Palo Alto, CA 94301
415-323-3378
w3.com
$4,995

Visitor-tracking software designed for UNIX platforms. Simultaneously tracks Web site visitors and tailors site content and advertising to their individual needs.

SERVICES

NetCount Basic and NetCount Plus
NetCount
1645 North Vine Street, Level 4
Los Angeles, CA 90028
213-848-5700
www.netcount.com
NetCount Basic, free; NetCount Plus, from $195 per month to more than $1,395 per month, depending on number of hits the Web site receives
Provides information about traffic to Web sites including who is visiting, how much time is spent and what they are looking at. Compares the Web site's effectiveness to others in its business category.

Nielsen I/PRO I/COUNT and Nielsen I/PRO I/AUDIT
Internet Profiles Corporation (I/PRO)
785 Market Street, 13th Floor
San Francisco, CA 94103
415-975-5800
www.ipro.com
I/COUNT from $200 to $6,000 monthly; I/AUDIT from $1,500 to $3,000 for monthly or quarterly reports
Measurement and evaluation services for the Internet. I/COUNT is a Web measurement system allowing site owners to monitor total numbers of visits, sec-

tions read within the site, and geographic and organizational origin of visitors. I/AUDIT is an auditing and verification system. Customers receive monthly or quarterly reports detailing Web audience usage and characteristics.

Processing Transactions

WEB SITES

CommerceNet
www.commerce.net
A trade organization dedicated to building commerce on the Web; offering tips and resources for processing online sales.

Security First Network Bank
www.sfnb.com
Provides online banking.

SOFTWARE, HARDWARE, AND SERVICES

CARI (Collect All Relevant Information)
Online Business Associates
1 Landmark Square
Stamford, CT 06901
203-969-3333
www.netresource.com
Call for pricing
Allows customers to purchase goods and services over the Web without exposing their credit card numbers to computer hackers. With the system, customers obtain a "virtual credit card number" that is useless to hackers. The actual credit card number never goes online and is stored in a secure computer that's inaccessible from the Internet.

Checkfree
Checkfree Corporation
8275 North High Street
Columbus, OH 43235
800-532-9696
www.checkfree.com

Free to merchants and consumers

Working with your bank, this transaction service allows consumers to pay using any credit card.

CyberCash

CyberCash, Inc.

2100 Reston Parkway, Suite 430

Reston, VA 22091

415-594-0800

www.cybercash.com

Free to merchants

Software payment system for secure Internet transactions among consumers, merchants, banks, and individuals. Links the Internet to the banking networks as needed. Handles credit card, debit, and cash transactions. Works with any Web browser or server by calling customers to download a free software module. The software module communicates with CyberCash's servers, which in turn communicate with the bank's private networks.

E-cash

Digicash

55 E. 52nd St., 27th Floor

New York, NY 10055-0186

212-909-4092

www.digicash.com

Free to merchants

Provides e-cash in an "electronic wallet" for individuals to store on a personal hard drive and authenticates the e-cash with merchants. Users can send money to a bank through a credit card or automated teller transaction, and the bank sends the user an equivalent amount of e-cash as an encrypted email message.

First Virtual Holdings

11975 El Camino Real, Suite 300

San Diego, CA

800-570-0003

www.firstvirtual.com

Account costs $10 to set up; for use in selling information, rather than handling orders. Company handles storage, distribution, and billing for 29 cents per transaction, plus 2 percent of transaction value.

First Virtual's electronic transaction system is based on email, not on specialized client software. A First Virtual customer opens an account and is given a confidential identification number. When the user wishes to buy a product or service, they send an E-mail message containing the identification number to the merchant. The merchant sends the ID number to First Virtual by E-mail for verification and identification of the customer. First Virtual then confirms with the customer by E-mail.

iCat Electronic Commerce Toolkit
Interactive Catalog Corporation
1420 Fifth Avenue #800
Seattle, WA 98101
206-623-0977
www.icat.com
Introductory price of $1,499 for Publisher and Commerce Exchange; normally $4,995 for three products, including CD reader
Trio of products for creating and delivering customized interactive catalogs on CD-ROM or the Internet, and processing electronic transactions from either source.

ICVerify
ICVerify, Inc.
473 Rowland Way
Oakland, CA 94621
510-553-7500
info@icverify.com
$349 single user, $499 multi-user
PC-compatible credit card authorization software for use in Internet commerce; supports more than 80 card networks and allows access to 99 percent of U.S. banks.

Netscape Secure Commerce Server
Netscape Communications
501 East Middlefield Road
Mountain View, CA 94043
415-254-1900
$5,000
www.netscape.com
Netscape formed an alliance with First Data's electronic funds unit to create an online payment system. They have licensed public key encryption technology from RSA Data Security to provide secure transaction capabilities. Transactions are credit card based. Requires the use of Netscape browser.

Open Market Online Mall
Open Market Inc.
245 First Street
Cambridge, MA 02142
617-621-9500
www.openmarket.com
$50 per month
Store Builder option lets businesses create their own pages. Use of software is free, but order processing charge is $50 per month.

PGP (Pretty Good Privacy) Encryption Software
ViaCrypt
2104 W. Peoria Avenue
Phoenix, AZ 85029
602-944-0773
viacrypt@acm.org
Free consumer versions available online. Dowload sites can be found by using a search engine to browse with the keywords "pretty good privacy."
Commercial Version 4.0, $129 single user; business edition, $149 single user
Very secure public domain encryption algorithm. Version of PGP for MS-DOS and other UNIX platforms.

Quarterdeck WebSTAR/SSL Security Toolkit
StarNine Technologies, A Quarterdeck Corporation Company
13160 Mindanao Way
Marina del Rey, CA 90292
310-309-3700
www.quarterdeck.com
$1,295
System that can be added to any Web site on the Internet or an internal corporate network, enabling companies to offer secure Web transactions and document transfers. Product includes an encryption-enabled version of StarNine's Web server for the Macintosh and utilities for creating a digital ID for the server.

Using the Internet for Profit
CD Solutions, Inc.
111 Speen Street
Framingham, MA 01701
508-879-0006
www.cdsolutions.com

$29.95

Self-directed CD-ROM using live sessions and a reference library; providing instruction on how small and home-based businesses can profit from the Internet.

VeriSign Digital IDs
VeriSign, Inc.
100 Marine Parkway
Redwood City, CA 94065
415-961-8820
www.verisign.com
$670
Hardware used with IBM's WebExplorer Browser and Internet Connection Secure Server that authenticates user identity and ensures privacy.

WebSite Professional
O'Reilly & Associates Inc.
103 Morris Street, Suite A
Sebastopol, CA 95472
800-998-9938
www.ora.com
$1,499
Web server security, including digital signatures and privacy for the exchange of payment information, personal identification, and intellectual property.

WebTrader 2.0
SBT Internet Systems Inc.
1401 Los Gamos Drive
San Rafael, CA 94903
415-444-9900
$1,295 source code version; $895 compiled version
Provides secure internet transactions using RSA Data's encryption security

PUBLICATIONS

Build a Worldwide Web Commerce Center by net.Genesis Corporation
John Wiley & Sons Inc.
605 Third Avenue
New York, NY 10158
212-850-6000

www.wiley.com/compbooks
$29.95
Comprehensive guide to technology and the business processes of conducting secure transactions on the Web.

Digital Money by Daniel C. Lynch and Leslie Lundquist
John Wiley & Sons Inc.
605 Third Avenue
New York, NY 10158
212-850-6000
www.wiley.com/compbooks
$24.95
Overview of the key players and technology of Internet commerce. Analyzes key issues, processes, and strategies to consider when assessing whether to set up a digital exchange system.

Appendix 5
• • • • • • • • • • •

Small Business Resource Web Sites

There are many small business sites run by consulting firms. Some of those sites are helpful; some are just teasers focused on signing up new clients. Those sites also rise and fall on a daily basis. Here, the focus is on more established sites that offer solid information to small businesses. To find additional sites, search by the keywords "small business" or "entrepreneur" on a search engine like Lycos or Yahoo!. To visit these sites, type in the address in the "location" field of your browser software. For some software, the code "http://" will have to be entered at the beginning of the address. Bear in mind that the Web is constantly changing, and some of these sites might be temporarily unavailable, might have moved to a new location with a new address, or changed their format or content.

The Cyberpreneur's Guide to the Internet
asa.ugl.lib.umich.edu/chdocs/cyberpreneur/Cyber.html
A comprehensive listing of links to useful business-related Web sites and other Internet resources for entrepreneurs.

Dun & Bradstreet
www.dbisna.com
Information on global marketing, strategic planning, job searches, marketing, and industry trend information. Companies can apply for a D-U-N-S number at the site.

Entrepreneurial Edge Online
www.edgeonline.com
Part of the Edward Lowe Foundation, this site has databases of resources, plus tips and advice organized into modules that cover starting, growing, and marketing a new business. It also has other resources like conference listings and links to other sites.

e-land
www.e-land.com
Lists the top ten business sites, software and print resources, and gives advice on how to maintain a Web site.

Entrepreneurs Web Page
sashimi.wwa.com/~notime/eotw/EOTW.html
Listings of resources by region, and a collection of links to other helpful Web sites for entrepreneurs.

Government Resources
www.govcon.com
One stop to find local, state, and federal government regulations, free access to the Commerce Business Daily, databases, contractors, and more.

Hoover's Company Directory
www.hoovers.com
Directory of information about public and private companies worldwide.

Inc.
www.inc.com
Browsable databases of back issues of Inc. and Inc. Technology, plus links to other sites and a simple form for creating a Web site to be stored on the magazine's server.

IOMA
www.ingress.com/ioma
The Web's best roundup of links to Internet business resources organized by management discipline, including a section on small business.

Lexis-Nexis Small Business Advisor
lex-nex.openmarket.com/lexis-nexis/db/welcosbs.html
Fee-based reprints of published articles from a number of magazines and newspapers, organized by topic and available through keyword search.

PhoNETic
www.soc.qc.edu/phonetic
Find out what catchy phrases match given phone numbers by typing the phone number into an on-site form—or find what phone numbers match a given phrase.

Small Business Administration
www.sbaonline.sba.gov
Listing of SBA publications, reports, and regional offices, this site delivers complete information that businesses normally have to request by phone or mail.

Small Business News
www.sbnpub.com
A monthly posting of selected stories from Small Business News Publications, browsable by geographic region. Also a listing of "briefs" by management discipline.

Small Business Survival Committee
www.sbsc.org
SBSC is a nonpartisan, nonprofit free-market organization that works to roll back the tax and regulatory demands on small business and entrepreneurs.

U.S. Chamber of Commerce
www.cais.com/chamber
Local, regional, and small business programs.

Wall Street Journal
www.wsj.com
Daily versions of the *Wall Street Journal* online, plus free money and investing update reports.

The White House
www.whitehouse.gov
Send a letter to the president.

Yahoo!'s Small Business Information
www.yahoo.com/Business_and_Economy/Small_Business_Information
Yahoo!'s search engine narrows its scope to find topics relevant only to small businesses. There are also subdirectories, like "venture capital," that list Web sites focusing on financing small businesses.

Appendix 6
•••••••••••

Companies Profiled in Case Studies

Chapter 1

The Virginia Diner
P.O. Box 310
Wakefield, VA 23888
800-868-6887
www.infi.net/vadiner

TSI Soccer
1408-A Christian Avenue
Durham, NC 27705
800-842-6679
919-383-4363
www.tsisoccer.com/tsi/index.html

CLAM Associates
101 Main Street
Cambridge, MA 02142
617-621-2542
www.clam.com

Chapter 2

October Films
65 Bleecker Street, 2nd Floor
New York, NY 10012
212-539-4000
www.octoberfilms.com

electronic Gourmet Guide
P.O. Box 3407
Crestine, CA 92325
909-338-7040
www.2way.com/food

Personal Creations
530 Executive Drive
Willowbrook, IL 60521
708-655-3200
cybermart.com/personalize.com/gift

Chapter 3

Copytech
1020 Turnpike Street
Canton, MA
617-828-7500
www.copytech.com

Aleph
350 Townsend Street #424A
San Francisco, CA 94107
415-512-1112
www.aleph.com

Lab-Beta
660 West Guiberson Road
Filmore, CA 93015
805-522-2382
E-mail address: donbush@earthlink.net

Bluestone Consulting
1000 Briggs Road
Mt. Laurel, NJ 08054
609-727-4600
www.bluestone.com

Park City Group
333 Main Street
Park City, UT 84060
801-645-2105
www.parkcity.com

Chapter 4

Oak Ridge Public Relations
21771 Stevens Creek Boulevard, Suite 203
Cupertino, CA 95014
408-253-5042
www.oakridge.com

Univenture
4707 Roberts Road
Columbus, OH 43228
614-529-2100
www.univenture.com

Advanced Hardware Architectures, Inc.
2365 NE Hopkins Court
Pullman, WA 99163
509-334-1000
www.aha.com

Operational Technologies
4100 NW Route 410
San Antonio, TX 78227
210-731-0000
www.otcorp.com

Sweetwater Sound
5335 Bass Road

Fort Wayne, IN 46808
219-432-8176
www.sweetwater.com

White Rabbit Toys
2611 Plymouth Road
Ann Arbor, MI 48105
313-665-1555
www.toystore.com

Chapter 5

PhotoDisk
2013 Fourth Avenue
Seattle, WA 98121
800-528-3472
www.photodisc.connectinc.com

Zaske, Sarafa and Associates
355 S. Woodward, Suite 200
Birmingham, MI 48009
810-647-5990
www.zsa.com

Tennis Warehouse
778 Higuera Street
San Luis Obispo, CA 93401
805-781-6464
www.calamer.com/tw

Chapter 6

Hot Hot Hot
56 Lacey Street
Pasadena, CA 91105
818-564-1090
www.hothothot.com

Alberto's Nightclub
736 W. Dana Street
Mountain View, CA 94040
415-968-3007
www.albertos.com

Virtual Reality Labs
2341 Ganador Court
San Luis Obispo, CA 93401
805-545-8515
www.vrli.com/vrli

Avweb
InterNetwork Publishing Corp.
5455 N. Federal Highway, Suite O
Boca Raton, FL 33487
407-989-9330
www.avweb.com

Forsyth Dental Center
140 Fenway
Boston, MA 02115
617-262-5200
www.forsyth.org

Chapter 7

Lasermax
3495 Winton Place, Building B
Rochester, NY 14623
716-272-5420
www.lasermax.com

PhotoCollect
740 West End Avenue
New York, NY
212-222-7381
www.webart.com/photocollect

Cattron, Inc.
58 West Shenango Street

Sharpsville, PA 16150
412-962-3571
www.industry.net/cattron

Sonnet Software
135 Old Cove Road, Suite 203
Liverpool, NY 13090
315-453-3096
www.sonnetusa.com

Eurosport
431 US Highway 70-A East
Hillsborough, NC 27278
919-644-6800
www.soccer.com

Chapter 8

Select Comfort
6105 Trenton Lane North
Minneapolis, MN 55442
612-551-7000
www.comfort.com

Windham Hill Records
P.O. Box 9388
Stanford, CA 94309
415-329-0647
www.windham.com

Busey Bank
201 W. Main Street
Urbana, IL 61801
217-384-4500
www.busey.com

Chapter 9

Virtual Vineyards
3803 E. Bayshore Road

Palo Alto, CA 94303
415-938-9463
www.virtualvin.com

EquiSearch
Box 553
Westerly, RI 02891
401-348-0025
www.equisearch.com

electronic *Gourmet Guide*
P.O. Box 3407
Crestline, CA 92325-3407
909-338-7040
www.2way.com.80/food

Aircraft Shopper Online
5725 Paradise Drive, Suite 200
Corte Madera, CA 94925
415-927-2255
www.aso.solid.com

Index

● ● ● ● ● ●

TEMP STN &
AOL. 6am